The Kingdom of God is Like This

DAVID H. van DAALEN

London
EPWORTH PRESS

7162 0261 1

Enquiries should be addressed to
The Methodist Publishing House
Wellington Road
Wimbledon
London SW19 8EU
Printed in Great Britain by
The Garden City Press Limited,
Letchworth, Hertfordshire SG6 1JS

The Kingdom of God is Like This

E Raymond Walker

Greenock '77.

Contents

Contents

Introduction

THERE is no doubt that the parables of Jesus belong to the best known and best loved stories of the New Testament. They are also the part of his teaching that seems to be least affected by questions as to whether or not he actually told them. True, like all the Lord's sayings, they were handed down by word of mouth, and they were repeated by the early Christians with a view to their own questions and their own needs. The effect of that can sometimes be seen quite clearly in the parables as we now have them. We must therefore not exaggerate the accuracy with which they were passed on, but on the whole we can say that they were handed down with remarkable fidelity.

However, whilst we can be reasonably certain that, if there is any reliable information about the Lord's teaching, it is to be found in the parables, there is no such certainty regarding their interpretation. In particular, there is a great gulf fixed between the traditional interpretation and use of the parables and the modern scholarly approach.

It has long been the custom to read the parables as allegories. *Allegory* means 'saying something else' and an allegory is a story in which everything stands for something else. Every detail has a hidden meaning, and if we want to understand such a story we must first decode it and find out what every detail stands for. An extreme example of such allegorical interpretation is Augustine's comment on the parable of the Good Samaritan (quoted here from C. H. Dodd, *The Parables of the*

7

Kingdom[1], who cites it as *the* example of how we should not read them).

> *A certain man went down from Jerusalem to Jericho*; Adam himself is meant; *Jerusalem* is the heavenly city of peace, from whose blessedness Adam fell; *Jericho* means the moon and signifies our mortality, because it is born, waxes, wanes and dies. *Thieves* are the devil and his angels. *Who stripped him*, namely, of his immortality; *and beat him*, by persuading him to sin; *and left him half-dead*, because in so far as man can understand and know God, he lives, but in so far as he is wasted and oppressed by sin, he is dead; he is therefore called *half-dead*. The *priest and Levite* who saw him and passed by, signify the priesthood and ministry of the *Old Testament*, which could profit nothing for salvation. *Samaritan* means Guardian, and therefore the Lord Himself is signified by this name. . . .

We need not really go any further. When we read the simple story as recorded by Luke, it seems perverse to apply such sophistication to its interpretation, and few people today would go to the same lengths as the more imaginative patristic and medieval interpreters. It is also obvious that this clever interpretation really obscures the point the Lord wanted to make when he told this parable: he was not giving instruction about the doctrine of salvation but about loving our neighbours as ourselves.

But to some extent the same method is still used, if not for the parable of the Good Samaritan, certainly for many others. In the parable of the Lost Sheep, for instance, we are told that the sheep stands for the sinner, the ninety-nine are the self-righteous Pharisees, and the shepherd is God, or perhaps Christ. As we shall see (p. 89) the point of the parable is precisely that we are not sheep, but nevertheless a good listener can learn something about God from it.

The man who has done most to draw the attention to the fact that the parables are not allegories was A. Jülicher, whose book, *Die Gleichnisreden Jesu*[2] has influenced all that has been written about the parables since. One of his main theses is that in every parable there is one point of comparison, and one point only. While in an allegory every detail has to be inter-

[1] Nisbet, London 1961, pp. 1–2; Fontana Books, 1961, p. 13.
[2] Tübingen, 1910.

preted, a parable does not demand any such detailed interpretation. In a parable only one point matters, and all that we have to do is to find out what that one point is.

That may sound all right to a man sitting at his desk writing a learned book about the parables, but it is not so obvious to someone just reading one of them for himself or for a preacher preparing a sermon and trying to find a suitable illustration. Can we really imagine the Lord saying to himself, 'Now I must remember that I am telling a parable and not an allegory, so I must make sure that none of the details could possibly mean anything'?

It is true that the parables were told to drive one particular point home, and it is therefore necessary for us to grasp the point. But it would surely be too pedantic to insist that therefore every detail must be irrelevant.

A parable is first and foremost a story. In that respect the parables differ from the kind of figurative speech which the Gospel according to John records so frequently. Even so, in a story every detail counts not because 'it stands for something' but simply because it adds to the picture. Whether or not it also affects the interpretation or the application of the parable must surely be ascertained from case to case.

A parable is a story: that is where it differs from figurative speech. But we must go further. It is *just* a story: that is where it differs from an allegory. An allegory is also a story, but in it every detail is governed by the interpretation, and without the interpretation the story is meaningless. Take, for instance, the opening scene of Bunyan's *Pilgrim's Progress*. There is a man standing outside a house, with a book in his hand and a great burden on his back. A little later we are told that he is 'undone by reason of a burden that lieth hard upon me'. Why does he not just lay it down? In a real story that would have been the obvious thing to do. But this is not an ordinary story, and the burden stands for the load of his sin, which can be shed only when he comes to the Cross. This feature would be quite absurd in a real story: it becomes meaningful only through its interpretation.

By way of contrast look at the war between Lilliput and Blefescu in the first part of Swift's *Gulliver's Travels*. There can be little doubt that the author was hinting at the futile wars between Britain and France. But the story remains meaningful in itself and can be read and enjoyed by anyone who may have no idea that the author was doing anything other than just spinning a yarn. Indeed, the book is full of reflections of Swift's own world and contains some biting criticism of the contemporary scene. But nothing in the stories 'stand for something else': everything remains within the context of the tale. There is no allegory here.

For a right understanding of the parables we ought to remember that the first listeners heard them just as stories. But they were stories meant to make them sit up and take notice.

Moreover, they were told to particular people in a particular situation. They were not fables illustrating a general truth but spotlights on a particular situation. Unfortunately that situation is not always known. These stories were handed down without contexts, often without any indication as to when they were spoken and to whom. The Evangelists seem to have been aware of their connexion with specific situations, and have sometimes created a suitable context for them. They have generally done that with a sound understanding of what each parable wants to convey, but we cannot always be certain that every parable was first told in the kind of context in which we now find it. Indeed, the Evangelists do not always agree on that point. For instance, Matthew and Luke put the parable of the Lost Sheep in quite different situations (Matthew 18:10–14; Luke 15:1–7). That seems to indicate that their source contained no information as to when and where Jesus told the story, and to whom. Of course, it is possible that he told it more than once. Every preacher who has a good story will use it again and again if the occasion arises. But in this case it seems pretty certain that Matthew and Luke found the story in the same source, which evidently did not refer to the situation. Even if the Lord did tell this parable on more than one occasion, the situations described in the Gospels were created by the Evangelists.

On the other hand, the Lord was not only a great story-teller. He knew exactly what he wanted to convey, and the parables contain adequate hints at the point he wanted to make. If we try to read the parables as if we had never heard them before—not an easy task, this—we should be able to see what he was driving at.

How then do we read the parables? It may be helpful to remember that they have travelled a certain distance before they reached us.

1. First of all Jesus told the parables to certain specific people in view of specific circumstances; and he did it to drive home a certain point.

2. After that they were handed down by word of mouth within the Christian community. However, that was not done because of any historical interest. These were not the words of a dead teacher but those of the living Lord. It was, of course, extremely interesting to know what the Lord had said to the people who listened to him while he was in the flesh, but it was much more important to know what he had to say to those who were now listening to him after his resurrection. The parables had to be told in such a way that they could be meaningful to this new generation. That does not mean that they were altered deliberately to suit the needs of this new generation; yet these needs were always in the minds of those who passed on the Lord's preaching and teaching and were therefore bound to affect the tradition.

3. The Evangelists, when they wrote the Gospels, were giving a portrait of the Lord, his words and his actions while he was in the flesh. One of the first problems in recording his words would be that these would often have been handed down by themselves, without any context. In a book, however, some context would have to be given. It would therefore be necessary to visualize the kind of situation in which these words would be meaningful. But their aim was not purely historical, but ultimately to show what the living Christ was like. Like those who had preserved the oral tradition before them they did not want to write about a dead hero. They wanted to present a risen and living Lord: here he is, this is what he is like. Therefore when relating the parables they did not aim to show what every one of them meant, or was intended to mean, to those who first heard them, but to make sure that they should be meaningful to the readers. They were convinced that the Lord

wanted to speak, not only to those who had listened to him in the past in Galilee or in Jerusalem, but also to the present generation, to those who were going to read their books. These, after all, were the words of their living Lord. The readers were not to remain mere spectators, they were to be involved, they were to become partners in conversation with the Lord.

4. The history of the parables did not stop there. Once the four Gospels had been accepted by the Church, their actual wording became fixed, but the interpretation continued to be affected by changing needs and attitudes which, however, we need not discuss.

5. The modern critic has the task of examining the first three stages. As far as possible he must discard the later history of their interpretation and start from the parables as he finds them in the Gospels. But he must try, if he can, to work backwards from there and to find out how they were first told and what they were meant to convey to those who first heard them. It would be dishonest to do otherwise. True, work of this kind is never finished, and the answers we find to our questions are never final. As in all human knowledge there is always an element of uncertainty. But if we disregard the original context and forms we can read into the parables whatever we like, and in the end we will no longer be listening to the Lord but just indulging our own fertile imaginations.

6. Ultimately, however, we will miss the goal if we merely ask questions about the past. We cannot do without a thorough critical investigation of the parables, not if we want to be honest. Of course, we cannot all work on what is, after all, a specialist job, but we can at least listen to those who have made it their field of study. But if Jesus Christ is the living Lord, then it is not enough to watch him speaking to people of long ago: we must listen to him speaking to us now. We cannot remain mere spectators, we must become partners with him in conversation, we must hear what he is saying to us now through the stories he told then.

The parables are not really difficult. What makes them difficult to us is the presence of so many layers of interpretation. They have become like old paintings with several layers of yellowed varnish, so that we can no longer see the brilliance of the original colours. They need cleaning, so that we can see them again in their original brilliance and simplicity. That may be a difficult and painful process: painful because we had become attached to the dim religious light, and difficult because we may discover under the varnish that the masterpiece has been touched up by hands other than the Master's. But it is something worth doing, for it makes it possible for us again to see and to hear not what generations of clever or not so clever interpreters had to say, but what the Master himself wants to say to us.

1

The Kingdom of God is Right Here

MARK, the earliest of the Evangelists, sums up the Lord's teaching in the words, 'The time is fulfilled, and the kingdom of God is at hand; repent, and believe in the gospel' (Mark 1:15). The translation contains an element of interpretation: the meaning of the Greek is, 'the Kingdom of God has approached'. As Mark saw it, the implication was that the Kingdom of God had arrived. God was exercising his royal government through Jesus.

However, Mark was aware this was by no means obvious, and he explains it by his theology of the messianic secret. The mystery of the Kingdom of God is hidden from those outside. The parables play an important part in that: 'To you has been given the secret of the kingdom of God, but for those outside everything is in parables' (Mark 4:11). That does not mean that Mark thought the Lord spoke in riddles. He knew that there was nothing deliberately obscure in the parables (Mark 4:13). But the parables do bring about a division between those who do and those who do not respond, which is what they were designed to do. They do not just *show* the difference between good and bad listeners: they *create* a division between those who recognize what God is doing in Jesus Christ and those who do not.

The point is not simply that people cannot understand the parables referring to the Kingdom of God. It is rather that the Kingdom, or, rather, the King, has arrived, but incognito. Jesus does not look like the Christ, the Messiah, the King, and,

15

indeed, he does not say openly that he is. But make no mistake about it, God rules through him and his plans cannot fail.

Mark's messianic secret is, of course, a particular interpretation of the Lord's ministry, and to some it may seem to be no more than a rather artificial construction. However, the value of his interpretation can only be judged fairly by an examination of the evidence. If it is true that the coming of Jesus means that the Kingdom of God has approached, but incognito, then we would expect some reference to that in the Lord's preaching and teaching. And, indeed, there are a number of parables which make precisely this point: do not be deceived by appearances, the Kingdom of God is right here.

The Sower

Again he began to teach beside the sea. And a very large crowd gathered about him, so that he got into a boat and sat in it on the sea; and the whole crowd was beside the sea on the land. And he taught them many things in parables, and in his teaching he said to them:

'Listen! A sower went out to sow. And as he sowed, some seed fell along the path, and the birds came and devoured it. Other seed fell on rocky ground, where it had not much soil, and immediately it sprang up, since it had no depth of soil; and when the sun rose it was scorched, and since it had no root it withered away. Other seed fell among thorns and the thorns grew up and choked it, and it yielded no grain. And other seeds fell into good soil and brought forth grain, growing up and increasing and yielding thirtyfold and sixtyfold and a hundredfold.'

And he said, 'He who has ears to hear, let him hear.'

(Mark 4:1–9)

That same day Jesus went out of the house and sat beside the sea. And great crowds gathered about him, so that he got into a boat and sat there; and the whole crowd stood on the beach. And he told them many things in parables, saying:

'A sower went out to sow. And as he sowed, some seeds fell along the path, and the birds came and devoured them. Other seeds fell on rocky ground, where they had not much soil, and immediately they sprang up, since they had no depth of soil, but when the sun rose they were scorched; and since they had no root they withered away. Other seeds fell upon thorns, and the thorns grew up and choked

them. Other seeds fell on good soil and brought forth grain, some a hundredfold, some sixty, some thirty. He who has ears, let him hear.'
(Matthew 13:1–9)

And when a great crowd came together and people from town after town came to him, he said in a parable:
'A sower went out to sow his seed; and as he sowed, some fell along the path, and was trodden under foot, and the birds of the air devoured it. And some fell on the rock; and as it grew up, it withered away, because it had no moisture. And some fell among thorns; and the thorns grew with it and choked it. And some fell into good soil and grew, and yielded a hundredfold.'
And as he said this, he called out, 'He who has ears to hear, let him hear.'
(Luke 8:4–8)

The parable of the Sower is one of the few that have been handed down with an interpretation, or, rather, with two interpretations. The first of these (Mark 4:10–12; Matthew 13:10–17; Luke 8:9–10; see pp. 20–22) consists of some sayings of Jesus which the Evangelists regarded as relevant to the parables in general and this one in particular; the second (Mark 4:14–20; Matthew 13:18–23; Luke 8:11–15; see pp. 22–24) seems to treat the parable as an allegory and, in its present form at least, can scarcely be attributed to the Lord himself.

Difficult though this may be—for most of us have been used to the added interpretation since we first heard the parable—it is advisable to look at the story just as Jesus told it. Unfortunately we no longer know precisely in what circumstances it was first told. The information supplied by Mark is not sufficient for us to know exactly how the listeners looked upon the Lord and his ministry. We just have the parable as it stands, and we shall have to interpret it from its content only.

If we try to put ourselves in the position of an unsuspecting hearer who has no clue as to the interpretation, we must first realize that the sower is just a sower, the seed is just seed, the soil is just soil, etc. What then is the striking point about the story? Ask any child that has not heard it before, and the answer is almost invariably, 'That farmer is daft'. They have a point. Who in his right senses would waste three parts of his precious seed in the manner described in the parable? Interpreters usually point out that farming methods in ancient Palestine were not very efficient and, particularly, that sowing was done before ploughing. A farmer would therefore not be able to see exactly where the rocky parts were, and he would sow on the path and among the thorns because they were to be ploughed under. That is all true enough, but even in ancient Palestine a farmer who wasted most of his seed would have been exceptional.

However, and this is surely a point that should be noted: that was what this particular piece of land was like. It so happens that this particular farmer has this particular field. It would have been nice if he had had a better field, but as things are he just has to work the piece of land that he has, a field with very little soil over the rock so that parts of it will yield no crop at all, a piece on the very edge of the cultivated land so that the thorns are forever encroaching on it, a piece that is cut in halves by an awkward right of way.

If we start there, with the unpromising field, we can see that the farmer is not so much foolish as persistent. A man with less stamina might have given up and perhaps tried his hand at begging—probably a more lucrative means of livelihood than trying to farm this awful piece of land.

Once we have seen that we can also see the point of the parable. The story ends with a surprise. Who would have thought it: the field yields an abundant harvest! The sower's effort was justified after all.

Looking at the parable with the Lord's ministry in mind, it is not difficult to see the connexion. We tend to think of the early part of his ministry as a huge success, with vast crowds following him. But what is success in terms of the Kingdom of God? All right, the common folk heard him gladly and he preached to large crowds. He was, after all, a powerful preacher and an extremely good story-teller and there cannot have been much other entertainment. But listening to him and saying, 'O how beautiful!' is not going to bring about the Kingdom of God. He does not want people's admiration: he wants them to follow him (cf. Matthew 7:21-9).

Like his preaching, other aspects of his ministry, however wonderful, did not produce results in terms of 'a successful ministry'. Our Lord certainly healed without any strings attached and he never took it for granted that a person who had been healed would become a disciple; in fact, he did not even ask them. But a story like Luke 17:11–9 shows how little appreciation his work could sometimes receive: out of ten lepers cured of their disease only one bothered to thank him and to praise God.

This was his field: an unreceptive and unresponsive people. The various kinds of soil are, of course, merely illustrations of what a farmer might find in a poor field; they were not, originally, meant to indicate various kinds of people. But the total picture of an unpromising field of labour points to the Lord's own unpromising ministry. Nevertheless, he knows that the harvest will be abundant.

Was the parable first told to encourage the disciples?—do not be discouraged by appearances, my ministry will bear fruit! Or was it told to warn the crowds?—do not be deceived by appearances, I am carrying out God's plan! Who can tell? But in either case the point is the same. The Lord's ministry may not be much to look at; it may not seem very promising: but the outcome will be beyond the wildest dreams, beyond the most extravagant hopes. This is not, however, merely a statement of the Lord's confidence: it is an appeal to the listeners, whether disciples or others, to recognize what God is doing through him, to see God at work in him.

This parable is not a symbolic statement of a general truth: it is an appeal to listeners in a particular situation during the Lord's ministry. But it is obvious that its message can be applied to similar situations facing those who share in the Lord's ministry. The ministry of the Gospel often seems a waste of time. Measured by standards of success it often seems to be extremely unproductive. Most people actively engaged in that ministry have experienced that. Like everybody else they like to see the results of their work, but it may be a long time before they do. As one minister once expressed it, 'In my sort of work we cannot expect to see the results until the next life—and that is an awfully long time to wait.' They are therefore faced with two temptations. One is to try to 'win the world for Christ' by any means available, whether it be by adopting methods of high-pressure evangelism which bring instant results, even though these results are often short-lived, or by adapting the Gospel to the needs, or, rather, the desires of the people. The other temptation is that of giving up altogether. But Christian obedience must not be measured by the immediate results. The outcome is in God's hands, and the harvest will be abundant. This parable can thus become a source of encouragement for discouraged servants of Christ.

Indeed, it is not only in the ministry of the Gospel in that direct sense that Christians meet discouragement. There is much Christian effort that seems to lead nowhere. Christian love often meets with no response. Christian concern for others is often met with hostility. Christian attempts to relieve suffering frequently have no success. But obedience to Christ cannot be measured by immediate results. And so here too this parable can be a source of much needed encouragement.

But we have to remember that this application is not the interpretation of the parable. It follows from it, but only inasmuch as the parable refers to Christ and we are following him. In the final resort it is he whose apparently wasted effort is in fact the accomplishing of God's purpose. Any application of the parable to ourselves must begin with recognizing him and his work, seeing what God is doing through him, and trusting God for the outcome. That is as necessary today as on that day when the Lord first preached the parable. Is not part of the Church's problem today that we are too concerned about the significance (or insignificance) of our work? Whatever we think, whatever we feel, whatever things may look like, the world's destiny was decided then, when Jesus came. You cannot see that? Of course not. It is in God's hands. But it is safe there.

And when he was alone, those who were about him with the twelve asked him concerning the parables. And he said to them,

'To you has been given the secret of the kingdom of God, but for those outside everything is in parables; so that they may indeed see but not perceive, and may indeed hear but not understand; lest they should turn again, and be forgiven.'

(Mark 4 : 10–12)

Then the disciples came and said to him, 'Why do you speak to them in parables?' And he answered them,

'To you it has been given to know the secrets of the kingdom of heaven, but to them it has not been given. For to him who has will more be given, and he will have abundance; but from him who has not, even what he has will be taken away. This is why I speak to them in parables, because seeing they do not see, and hearing they do not hear, nor do they understand. With them indeed is fulfilled the prophecy of Isaiah which says:

"You shall indeed hear but never understand,
and you shall indeed see but never perceive.
For this people's heart has grown dull,
and their ears are heavy of hearing,
and their eyes they have closed,
lest they should perceive with their eyes,
and hear with their ears,
and understand with their heart,
and turn for me to heal them."

But blessed are your eyes, for they see, and your ears, for they hear. Truly, I say to you, many prophets and righteous men longed to see what you see, and did not see it, and to hear what you hear, and did not hear it.'

(Matthew 13:10–17)

And when his disciples asked him what this parable meant, he said, 'To you it has been given to know the secrets of the kingdom of God; but for others they are in parables, so that seeing they may not see, and hearing they may not understand.'

(Luke 8:9–10)

The Evangelists add two interpretations. The first simply comments on the parables in general and this one in particular. The disciples have been given the secret, or, rather, the mystery of the Kingdom of God, but to other people everything is given in parables, so that they may see but not perceive, hear but not understand. That seems to suggest that it was the purpose of the parables that people should not understand, and that may well be what Mark had in mind. But was it also what Jesus had in mind? Surely, no one speaks in order that people may not understand him. The more reasonable interpretation is that the teaching of our Lord brings about a parting of the ways, and that is what it is meant to do. One cannot remain neutral listening to the Gospel. It demands a decision and consequently a division. It leads either to obedience or to disobedience, either

21

to faith or to unbelief. Spiritual insight and understanding, faith and obedience come from hearing the preaching of the Gospel; but so do spiritual blindness and misunderstanding, unbelief and disobedience.

It is unlikely that Jesus uttered these sayings in connexion with the parable of the Sower, but Mark has seen rightly that they are relevant.

Matthew has added some more sayings. The first of these is particularly striking. Those who have the open mind to listen will receive even more; those who do not have it will lose even what little understanding they do have. Mark records sayings to that effect in verses 21–5.

Luke has left out the clause, 'Lest they should turn again and be forgiven.' He evidently did not wish to give the impression that the offer of God's mercy was not open to all.

And he said to them,
'Do you not understand this parable? How then will you under-
stand all the parables? The sower sows the word. And these are the
ones along the path, where the word is sown; when they hear, Satan
immediately comes and takes away the word which is sown in them.
And these in like manner are the ones sown upon rocky ground, who,
when they hear the word, immediately receive it with joy; and they
have no root in themselves, but endure for a while; then, when
tribulation or persecution arises on account of the word, immediately
they fall away. And others are the ones sown among thorns; they
are those who hear the word, but the cares of the world, and the
delight in riches, and the desire for other things, enter in and choke
the word, and it proves unfruitful. But those that were sown upon
the good soil are the ones who hear the word and accept it and bear
fruit, thirtyfold and sixtyfold and a hundredfold.'

(Mark 4:13–20)

'Hear then the parable of the sower. When any one hears the word
of the kingdom and does not understand it, the evil one comes and
snatches away what is sown in his heart; this is what was sown along
the path. As for what was sown on rocky ground, this is he who
hears the word and immediately receives it with joy; yet he has no
root in himself, but endures for a while, and when tribulation or
persecution arises on account of the word, immediately he falls away.
As for what was sown among thorns, this is he who hears the word,
but the cares of the world and the delight in riches choke the word,
and it proves unfruitful. As for what was sown on good soil, this is

he who hears the word and understands it; he indeed bears fruit, and yields, in one case a hundredfold, in another sixty, and in another thirty.'

(Matthew 13:18–23)

'Now the parable is this: The seed is the word of God. The ones along the path are those who have heard; then the devil comes and takes away the word from their hearts, that they may not believe and be saved. And the ones on the rock are those who, when they hear the word, receive it with joy; but these have no root, they believe for a while and in time of temptation fall away. And as for what fell among the thorns, they are those who hear, but as they go on their way they are choked by the cares and riches and pleasures of life, and their fruit does not mature. And as for that in the good soil, they are those who, hearing the word, hold it fast in an honest and good heart, and bring forth fruit with patience.'

(Luke 8:11–15)

As it stands this second interpretation seems to be allegorical, and it is therefore usually assumed that it cannot have been given by Jesus. Moreover, these verses abound in words not used elsewhere in the Gospels, which seems to suggest that they were not composed by Mark; in other words, they must have been added some time after the Lord's ministry but before Mark wrote his Gospel.

However, that verdict rests on the assumption that this really is meant to be an interpretation of the parable. But is it? The curious thing is that these verses do not really interpret the parable at all. They elaborate on some of the attitudes that may interfere with listening to the Gospel and illustrate the kind of thing that may frustrate the Lord's ministry, but they do not point the actual message of the story. Precisely because they still guard the mystery of the Kingdom of God we cannot entirely rule out the possibility that they may reflect comments made by the Lord himself, though scarcely in their present form.

After all, what would be more natural, when people complained about not seeing the point of the parable, than that they should be urged to listen well, and that the speaker, whether Jesus himself or a later preacher, should elaborate on some of the things that might stand in the way of proper listening? Do not the different kinds of soil suggest some of the dangers to good listening? Of course, the three kinds of bad listeners are only examples, but they represent fairly common ways of responding, or, rather, not responding to the challenge of the Gospel.

This is perfectly legitimate. Even if these comments are not from the Lord himself, it was legitimate for any preacher to make such comments, and they are still legitimate for any reader who finds himself portrayed here. It is important how we listen; these verses rightly remind us of that, and if they can help anyone to overcome a natural inclination to listen badly, that is all to the good.

But this way of reading the parable is fraught with certain dangers. For one thing, the three attitudes of mind here criticized are only a few examples of bad listening, and one could think of others not mentioned here. Secondly, and this is much more serious, we might become so obsessed with the importance of the individual listener that we lose sight of the main purpose of the parable and forget the Lord and his work. It is important how we listen, but it is more important that in spite of the poor soil the harvest is abundant, that in spite of people's poor response, God's plan is brought to perfection in Jesus Christ.

There is a secret to this, and, indeed, to every parable. The interpretation of the parable still guards that secret. But it is not a secret to be puzzled out. It is Jesus Christ. He is behind the persistent loving labour on an unpromising field, and he is behind the abundant harvest.

The seed growing secretly

And he said,

'The kingdom of God is as if a man should scatter seed upon the ground, and should sleep and rise night and day, and the seed should sprout and grow, he knows not how. The earth produces of itself, first the blade, then the ear, then the full grain in the ear. But when the grain is ripe, at once he puts in the sickle, because the harvest has come.'

(Mark 4: 26–9)

This is the only parable recorded by Mark that was not

24

repeated either by Matthew or Luke. Nothing is said about the situation in which it was told, and it must therefore be interpreted from its content.

We can discount any interpretation that emphasizes the point of natural growth. Whenever we read in the Bible about what we would call 'natural growth', the emphasis is on the *wonder* of such growth. That, indeed, is true of the entire ancient world. Nature was regarded as wonderful and miraculous, if also capricious. In the Gentile world nature was regarded as divine precisely because of the awe and wonder with which people viewed it.

In the early Christian Church seed and harvest were often connected particularly with death and resurrection, and the point of the comparison was that the resurrection of the dead, like the harvest, was miraculous, an act of God that no one can comprehend. Paul, John and Clement of Rome refer to seed and harvest in that sense (I Corinthians 15:35–8; John 12:24; I Clement 24:4–5). Jewish rabbis too used seed and harvest figuratively of death and resurrection.

When Jesus therefore says that the earth 'produces of itself' the blade, the ear and finally the grain in the ear, he is not thinking in terms of the wonder of natural development and growth. He simply means that after sowing (and ploughing) the farmer has to wait for the time when the field is ready to be harvested, and the emphasis is on the surprise that a few dead seeds produce such an abundant harvest. Of course, we know that the seeds are not dead, but that is not the point. The point is the contrast between the small seed and the rich harvest.

That this was the point that the Evangelist wanted to emphasize is shown by the fact that he placed it side by side with the parable of the Mustard Seed (vv.30–2). There too the emphasis is on the smallness of the seed and the huge size, this time not of the harvest but of the plant. In Mark's Gospel these two parables are presented as a pair to drive home the same point.

What that point is seems pretty obvious. Christians in general, and preachers of the Gospel in particular, should not be discouraged by the present humble condition of the Church, and the apparent lack of success with which their work met. All they have to do is to sow the seed, and leave the outcome

25

to God. That may not always be easy. Most people like to see results from their work. Waiting for the resurrection means that we have an awfully long time to wait before we see any results! But have good courage. The outcome is certain. God gives an abundant harvest.

That seems a satisfactory interpretation of the parable. But is it what Jesus had in mind? Here we cannot be certain. Originally the story may have been told in reply to a feeling of impatience among the disciples. It must have seemed to them that the Lord was forever saying that the Kingdom of God was close by but seemed to be doing nothing actually to bring it about. Did he want to drive home to them that the Kingdom is not brought about by feverish activity but by God's work alone?

Or is it God who resembles the sower? For a long time it seems that God is doing nothing, that he just lets the world take its course, and then suddenly his time has come and miraculously he brings about the Kingdom. This interpretation seems to be contradicted by the words, 'he knows not how', but we must not forget that the man in the parable is just a man, and if God is meant to resemble him in one point that does not mean that he has to resemble him at every point.

Or again, was the parable a challenge to put in the sickle there and then? The preparations for the Kingdom had been made long ago. The nation of Israel had been waiting for centuries, and nothing much seemed to have happened. Now the time had come. Jesus was there, and he, indeed, *was* the Kingdom; the harvest was being gathered in.

All the various interpretations make valid points. Yet we have the impression that Mark was right in putting the emphasis on the contrast between the seed and the harvest. Whether it is God, or Jesus, or any preacher, who resembles the farmer, remains an open question. The reality of the Kingdom is such that a valid case can be made out for all three interpretations. It is true that Jesus seemed to be doing nothing about bringing about the Kingdom, at least not as the disciples —and others—understood it. It is true that God often seems to leave the world to its own devices. It is true that every preacher will have to wait for the resurrection of the dead before he can expect to see the fruits of his labour. But it is also true—and this is much more important—that God does indeed bring about the Kingdom. That is real life from the dead.

In the light of that point the words 'he knows not how', have a special significance. In a sense Christians have to live with an element of uncertainty. There is much that we do not know. God, however, does know.

Of course, in the parable these words refer quite naturally to the man who sowed the seed and then just waited. But there is no denying that in several of the parables of the Kingdom there is not only the contrast between the small thing in evidence and the great eventual outcome, but also the surprise that God does his work we do not know how. God is a God of surprises.

The mustard seed and the leaven

And he said,
'With what can we compare the kingdom of God, or what parable shall we use for it? It is like a grain of mustard seed, which, when sown upon the ground, is the smallest of all the seeds on earth; yet when it is sown it grows up and becomes the greatest of all shrubs, and puts forth large branches, so that the birds of the air can make nests in its shade.'

(Mark 4:30–2)

Another parable he put before them, saying,
'The kingdom of heaven is like a grain of mustard seed which a man took and sowed in his field; it is the smallest of all seeds, but when it has grown it is the greatest of shrubs and becomes a tree, so that the birds of the air come and make nests in its branches.'

(Matthew 13:31–2)

He said therefore,
'What is the kingdom of God like? And to what shall I compare it? It is like a grain of mustard seed which a man took and sowed in his garden; and it grew and became a tree, and the birds of the air made nests in its branches.'

(Luke 13:18–19)

This parable again emphasizes the contrast between the unimpressive first appearance and the magnificent outcome. Every word serves to show how tiny the seed is and how large the plant. There are actually smaller seeds but the mustard seed is small enough to serve the purpose of the parable. The plant probably meant is the *sinapis nigra*, an uncommon variety that does grow in the area and reaches a height of over ten feet. Birds are not actually likely to nest in it. The word that is usually translated 'making their nests' could also be used of perching or resting; however, in the earliest version, Mark's, the birds, whatever they do, nesting or resting, do it in its shade, not in its branches.

There are certain differences between their versions but all three Evangelists emphasize the contrast between the tiny seed and the huge plant, and that seems to be the most obvious interpretation of the parable. Jesus was not thinking of the contrast between the tiny early Church and its expansion in later years, which would seem a very obvious interpretation. He was simply contrasting his own unimpressive appearance with the unique and all-embracing real significance of his ministry.

In Mark's Gospel this parable forms a pair with that of the Seed growing secretly; both Matthew and Luke pair it with that of the Leaven. That seems to suggest that they both found it in another source other than Mark, and that the Mustard Seed and the Leaven were already combined in that other source. It is now generally assumed that Matthew and Luke knew the Gospel according to Mark, but that they also had access to another book that is now lost, which mainly consisted of sayings of Jesus. It is usually referred to as Q, from the German *Quelle* = 'source'.

> *He told them another parable.*
> *'The kingdom of heaven is like leaven which a woman took and hid in three measures of meal, till it was all leavened.'*
>
> (Matthew 13:33)

> *And again he said,*
> *'To what shall I compare the kingdom of God? It is like leaven which a woman took and hid in three measures of meal, till it was all leavened.'*
>
> (Luke 13:20–1)

The parable itself is simple enough. A small piece of leaven—

we would, of course, use yeast—is enough to leaven a large quantity of dough. The quantity mentioned, nearly five stone, has no significance beyond being huge. It is easy to see how this parable could be used to encourage the small early Church. They might be a small body in a vast world, but very little was needed to leaven the whole lump. That was an obvious and perfectly legitimate use of the parable; indeed, it still is.

But is it quite what the Lord had in mind? The answer must be, no. The contrast between the tiny piece of leaven and the huge quantity of dough is indeed the point of the parable, but it does not point primarily to the Church and her function in the world. It points straight to the Lord and his work. Who would think that a little bit of leaven would make the whole lot rise so that it will be ready for baking? But, of course, everybody knows that it does. Who would think that this Man Jesus would bring the whole of God's plan to perfection? But that is precisely what he does do.

Is it then a mistake to apply the parable to the small and insignificant Church and her place in God's plan? That depends on how we relate that to the initial meaning of the parable. It is not just anything you put in the dough that will make it rise. It has to be leaven or yeast or baking powder; that is to say, it has to be the proper ingredient. The proper ingredient in the Kingdom of God is Jesus Christ the King. No one else will do. The Church's confidence in the significance of her work is justified as long as it is confidence in Christ. We may confidently apply the parable to the small Church and her great place in God's plan, we may regard her as God's leaven in the world's great lump, so long as we remember that, properly speaking, Christ is the leaven.

And, of course, we must remember that we have been speaking figuratively, and that the application of the parable goes further than its interpretation. The woman in the parable is just a woman, the dough is just dough, and the leaven is just leaven. But just as everyone knows that a little leaven does the trick, so we know that Jesus Christ is the One who brings God's work to perfection. That was the certain hope by which the disciples lived, it was the certain hope of the early Church, and it can still be ours.

29

2

The Day of Judgment

THE coming of Christ brought the Kingdom of God quite near. It is right here, and the encounter with him is the critical confrontation with God. But most people are totally unprepared. A number of parables were told with specific reference to this.

The encounter with Christ is itself a day of judgment. 'He who believes in him is not condemned; he who does not believe is condemned already' (John 3:18). Those who reject Christ think that they are passing judgment on him, but they are, in fact, putting themselves under sentence. As we shall see it is not by chance that the Gospel according to John, the latest of the four, states this much more explicitly than the others.

To the minds of the early Christians the critical encounter with Christ would lead immediately to the Last Judgment. That, indeed, seemed implied in the Lord's own teaching, and it is not surprising that the early Church fervently awaited his speedy return and that Day of Judgment. Very soon therefore parables which had been told in view of the present encounter with Christ were applied to the Last Judgment, and the Synoptic Gospels are full of examples.

John's Gospel, however, was written at a time when the expectation of the Lord's imminent return was beginning to recede. The Last Judgment seemed far off. But the Evangelist was too keenly aware of the urgency of Lord's call to transfer the judgment to an indeterminate future. He knew that the encounter with Christ was itself the judgment. For parables, though, we have to look in the other Gospels.

31

The Kingdom of God is Like This

The doorkeeper, the burglar and the servants left in charge

'But of that day or that hour no one knows, not even the angels in heaven, nor the Son, but only the Father. Take heed, watch ... for you do not know when the time will come. It is like a man going on a journey, when he leaves home and puts his servants in charge, each with his work, and commands the doorkeeper to be on the watch. Watch therefore—for you do not know when the master of the house will come, in the evening, or at midnight, or at cockcrow, or in the morning—lest he come suddenly and find you asleep. And what I say to you I say to all: Watch.'   (Mark 13:32-7)

'Watch therefore, for you do not know on what day your Lord is coming. But know this, that if the householder had known in what part of the night the thief was coming, he would have watched and would not have let his house be broken into. Therefore you also must be ready; for the Son of man is coming at an hour you do not expect.

'Who then is the faithful and wise servant, whom his master has set over his household, to give them their food at the proper time? Blessed is that servant whom his master when he comes will find so doing. Truly, I say to you, he will set him over all his possessions. But if that wicked servant says to himself, "My master is delayed," and begins to beat his fellow servants, and eats and drinks with the drunken, the master of that servant will come on a day when he does not expect him and at an hour he does not know, and will punish him, and put him with the hypocrites; there men will weep and gnash their teeth.'   (Matthew 24:42-51)

'and be like men who are waiting for their master to come home from the marriage feast, so that they may open to him at once when he comes and knocks. Blessed are those servants whom the master finds awake when he comes; truly, I say to you, he will gird himself and have them sit at table, and he will come and serve them. If he comes in the second watch, or in the third, and finds them so, blessed are those servants! But know this, that if the householder had known at what hour the thief was coming, he would have been awake and would not have left his house to be broken into. You also must be ready; for the Son of man is coming at an hour you do not expect.'

Peter said, 'Lord, are you telling this parable for us or for all?'

And the Lord said,

'Who then is the faithful and wise steward, whom his master will set over his household, to give them their portion of food at the proper time? Blessed is that servant whom his master when he comes will find so doing. Truly I tell you, he will set him over all his possessions. But if that servant says to himself, "My master is delayed in coming," and begins to beat the menservants and the maidservants,

*and to eat and drink and get drunk, the master of that servant will
come on a day when he does not expect him and at an hour he does
not know, and will punish him, and put him with the unfaithful. And
that servant who knew his master's will, but did not make ready or
act according to his will, shall receive a severe beating. But he who
did not know, and did what deserved a beating, shall receive a light
beating. Every one to whom much is given, of him will much be
required; and of him to whom men commit much they will demand
the more.'*

(Luke 12:36–48)

We have here a number of short parables which all seem to
make the same point. The parable of the Doorkeeper is only
in Mark (13:34); that of the Thief is in Matthew and Luke
(Matthew 24:43; Luke 12:39). The parable of the Servants
left in charge is hinted at by a few words in Mark (13:34),
recorded in a much more extensive form by Luke (12:36–8)
and given in yet another version by both Matthew and Luke
(Matthew 24:45–51; Luke 12:42–6). Luke has also appended
some verses (47–8) of what may have been yet another parable.
All three Evangelists place the parables in the context of an
announcement of the *parousia*, the Lord's second coming. That
day will be a day of judgment, so be wide awake and watch; be
prepared at all times, for you do not know when to expect him.

The point in every case is the unexpectedness. The servants do
not know when the master is due to return; the householder does
not know when a burglar might break in. No other point
should be emphasized. More particularly, we should not try to
allegorize. That is obvious in the case of the burglar—no one
is surely going to suggest that the burglar stands for Christ—
but it is also true in the other parables. But can we be sure
that the Lord himself, when telling these parables, was referring
to the Last Judgment?

Those who regard that as unlikely usually raise the objection
that the people who first heard these parables would know
nothing about a second coming of the Christ. That is true
enough, but they were expecting the Day of the Lord, which
was to be a Day of Judgment. There can be no doubt that
when our Lord referred to judgment, both he and the listeners
would have the Day of Judgment in mind.

But there is one thing wrong with thinking about judgment

33

only in terms of the Last Judgment. The Last Judgment is something that is to come. No one knows when that day will be, but it always seems to be far in the future, not a thing to worry about just now. The teaching of the coming Day of Judgment can be a means of stressing the seriousness of human life: we shall have to account for what we have made of our opportunities. But it can also be used as a pretext for putting off necessary decisions. The final verdict will not be given until much later, so we need not worry about changing our lives or changing the society in which we live just now. Tomorrow is another day.

Christian preachers in later centuries have expressed that by saying that it makes no difference when the Last Judgment will be. We only live this present life once, and when we die we shall have to be ready for the judgment. Death can strike us any time, therefore live every day as if it were your last.

The Lord did not, as far as we know, put it quite in those terms. But he did want to emphasize that judgment was imminent. He did, indeed, speak of the Last Judgment, and he did say that it was close at hand. But, much more important, it is unexpected. Indeed, the judgment is now. The decision falls now, in the encounter with Christ. This is expressed explicitly in the Gospel according to John: 'He who believes in him is not condemned; he who does not believe is condemned already, because he has not believed in the name of the only Son of God' (John 3:18). It is also certainly implied in these parables.

However, it would be a mistake to attach too much importance to the question of whether the Lord referred to his own unexpected coming or to the unexpected moment of death or to the unexpected day of the Last Judgment. That might well divert our attention from the real point of these parables: Be awake and watch! Be ready for God now!

The parable of the Servants left in charge has been handed down in two forms (Mark 13:34a = Luke 12:36–8, and Matthew 24:45–51 = Luke 12:42–6). Luke, who records both versions, may well be right that we have here two parables. The second version seems to have been directed specifically at the religious leaders of the nation.

Luke has also added two verses (47–8) which make a distinction between those servants who do and those who do not know the master's wishes. This distinction seems to contrast the leaders of the nation, who knew the Law, with the people who did not know the Law. The Pharisees in particular used to look down upon the masses who were ignorant of the Law. The Lord points out that responsibility lies with those who do know what God requires. The others are not innocent. Ignorance is no excuse but it is an extenuating circumstance.

These two added points are valuable. Leadership entails responsibility. So does knowledge of God's will. The religious leaders of the nation carry a heavier burden of responsibility, both because they are in charge of others and because they know better than the others. Yet the point of the parables remains that they have to give an account of their actions now. The story in Matthew 24:45–51 and Luke 12:42–6 was addressed to a particular group of people, not those addressed in the other parables. But all groups are called to be awake and to watch, to be ready for God now, for the judgment is imminent.

The fig tree

> 'From the fig tree learn its lesson: as soon as its branch becomes tender and puts forth its leaves, you know that summer is near. So also, when you see these things taking place, you know that he is near, at the very gates.' (Mark 13:28–9)

> From the fig tree learn its lesson: as soon as its branch becomes tender and puts forth its leaves, you know that summer is near. So also, when you see all these things, you know that he is near, at the very gates.' (Matthew 24:32–3)

> And he told them a parable:
> 'Look at the fig tree, and all the trees; as soon as they come out in leaf, you see for yourselves and know that the summer is already near. So also, when you see these things taking place, you know that the kingdom of God is near.' (Luke 21:29–31)

Mark has placed this parable in a context that makes it clear that he understood it as referring to the *parousia*, the Lord's second coming, and the other Evangelists have followed him. This application seems pretty obvious, but it raises an awkward question. Did the Lord really want to say that we can see the Last Judgment coming?

The point of the parable, surely, is that in ordinary, everyday things we know what to look for. People in those days would not have a calendar hanging on the wall, and the farmers would just look at natural things to see how time was moving on. In any case, there are slight variations in the year of nature, and every farmer worth his salt knows exactly what the signs are of an early or a late spring or summer.

The same is true in relation to the spiritual life. We ought to know what to look for. People meeting Jesus ought to be able to see that the Kingdom of God has come close by.

The way the wind blows

> He also said to the multitudes,
> 'When you see a cloud rising in the west, you say at once, "A shower is coming"; and so it happens. And when you see the south wind blowing, you say, "There will be scorching heat"; and it happens. You hypocrites! You know how to interpret the appearance of earth and sky; but why do you not know how to interpret the present time?' (Luke 12:54–6)

This parable is very similar to the one about the Fig Tree. In ordinary, everyday things we know what to look for. Indeed, observant country people can often predict the weather with considerably more accuracy than the forecast of the meteorological office. Why then do people meeting Jesus not realize that the Kingdom of God has come close by?

The foolish and the wise virgins

> 'Then the kingdom of heaven shall be compared to ten maidens who took their lamps and went to meet the bridegroom. Five of them were foolish and five were wise. For when the foolish took their lamps, they took no oil with them; but the wise took flasks of oil with their lamps. As the bridegroom was delayed, they all slumbered and slept. But at midnight there was a cry, "Behold, the bridegroom! Come out to meet him." Then all those maidens rose

and trimmed their lamps. And the foolish said to the wise, "Give us some of your oil, for our lamps are going out." But the wise replied, "Perhaps there will not be enough for us and for you; go rather to the dealers and buy for yourselves." And while they went to buy, the bridegroom came, and those who were ready went in with him to the marriage feast; and the door was shut. Afterward the other maidens came also, saying, "Lord, lord, open to us." But he replied, "Truly, I say to you, I do not know you." Watch therefore, for you know neither the day nor the hour.'

(Matthew 25:1–13)

British people are familiar with the scene of a groom waiting at the church for the bride and her father. In many lands, however, it is customary for the groom to fetch the bride from her home to take her to wherever the ceremony is to take place. In ancient Israel the groom would go to the bride's home, where he would receive his bride with a certain amount of ceremony, and then take her to his own home for the wedding. The maidens in the parable are companions of the bride, bridesmaids we would call them. In this story we have to picture them as waiting outside the bride's house for the bridegroom to arrive, ready to join the procession as soon as it left for his house.

Matthew understood this parable as referring to the *parousia*, the Lord's second coming. The early Church was waiting eagerly for that day, but it seemed to be delayed. No wonder people's zeal would begin to flag, their hope would grow dim, their faith would be assailed by doubts. It was not easy for the Church to keep herself in readiness for her Lord. Yet there was need to be ready at all times, for the Day is sure to come, and no one knows when.

Obvious though that interpretation seemed to Matthew, it would not have been so obvious to the people who were listening when Jesus first told the parable. It seems therefore much more likely that he was not referring to his second but to his first coming. When he came, did he find Israel prepared, and ready to receive him? Some, indeed, were wise and received him, but many were foolish and did not recognize the advent of the Son of God.

That first moment is unrepeatable. However, Matthew was certainly right in perceiving that the parable can be applied

37

to new situations. Readiness for the Lord was not only required of those who met the Lord while he was in the flesh. It is required of all, whenever they meet Jesus. It must also be admitted that this parable is eminently suited to being applied to the Last Judgment.

We must however be aware of two pitfalls. One is the temptation to regard this parable as an allegory. The need to be ready is the point of the story, and we must not try to find out what every detail stands for. It is tempting to look upon the bridegroom as representing Christ. After all, he is sometimes referred to as 'the Bridegroom'. True, but only in figures of speech where the bride is the Church. The bride is not even mentioned in this parable: the groom's partner was not relevant to the point the Lord wanted to make.

Attempts have also been made to identify what the oil stands for. When a preacher speaks about this parable he will want to be specific; he will want to ask what precisely is lacking in the Church. He may speak of the lack of faith, or the poverty of the spiritual life, or the dimness of the Christian hope. Indeed, any reader may do that, ask what is lacking in the Church, what is lacking in my own life. That is not only legitimate, it is necessary: it is the thing that we must do, apply it to our own situation. The mistake so often made is not that people apply the parable to themselves and see their own failure to meet Christ at his time on his terms, but that, on the contrary, by allegorizing the Lord's words, they manage to find an interpretation that applies to others, not to themselves.

The parable is, however, just a story. The groom is a groom, the maidens are bridesmaids, the oil is oil. The point is simply that some were ready and others were not; and a good listener will ask himself, 'Am I ready?'

The second pitfall is that the application of the parable to the Last Judgment may well divert our attention from the urgency of the demand to be ready now. The Last Judgment is not yet, so why worry now? The warning is not superfluous, 'Watch therefore, for you know neither the day nor the hour.' Be ready for Christ always. Be ready for him now.

3

The Hour of Crisis

THE Kingdom of God is right here. Right now, as we meet Christ, we are standing before God. This is therefore the moment of crisis, when decisions have to be taken.

Strictly speaking the word crisis means 'judgment'; and the Day of Judgment is the time of crisis. But it has become customary to use the word crisis specifically for a situation of imminent danger, when things are in the balance and decisions have to be taken which will determine the outcome one way or the other. The encounter with Christ is eminently *the* hour of crisis, the moment when an immediate decision and immediate action are required, so it is not surprising that a number of parables emphasize that. The parable of the Ten Virgins has already spoken of the need for appropriate readiness and appropriate action. The following parables go further.

The wicked husbandmen

And he began to speak to them in parables.

'*A man planted a vineyard, and set a hedge around it, and dug a pit for the wine press, and built a tower, and let it out to tenants, and went into another country. When the time came, he sent a servant to the tenants, to get from them some of the fruit of the vineyard. And they took him and beat him, and sent him away empty handed. Again he sent to them another servant, and they wounded him in the head, and treated him shamefully. And he sent another, and him they killed; and so with many others, some they beat and some they killed. He had still one other, a beloved son; finally he sent him to them,* saying, "They will respect my son." But those tenants said to one another, "This is the heir; come, let us kill him, and the inheritance will be ours." And they took him and killed him, and cast him out of the vineyard. What will the owner of the vineyard do? He will come and destroy the tenants, and give the vineyard to others.'

(Mark 12:1–9)

'Hear another parable. There was a householder who planted a vineyard, and set a hedge around it, and dug a wine press in it, and built a tower, and let it out to tenants, and went into another country. When the season of fruit drew near, he sent his servants to the tenants, to get his fruit; and the tenants took his servants and beat one, killed another, and stoned another. Again he sent other servants, more than the first; and they did the same to them. Afterward he sent his son to them, saying, "They will respect my son." But when the tenants saw the son, they said to themselves, "This is the heir; come, let us kill him and have his inheritance." And they took him and cast him out of the vineyard, and killed him. When therefore the owner of the vineyard comes, what will he do to those tenants?'
They said to him, 'He will put those wretches to a miserable death, and let out the vineyard to other tenants who will give him the fruits in their seasons.'

(Matthew 21:33–41)

And he began to tell the people this parable:
'A man planted a vineyard, and let it out to tenants, and went into another country for a long while. When the time came, he sent a servant to the tenants, that they should give him some of the fruit of the vineyard; but the tenants beat him, and sent him away empty-handed. And he sent another servant; him also they beat and treated shamefully, and sent him away empty-handed. And he sent yet a third; this one they wounded and cast out. Then the owner of the vineyard said, "What shall I do? I will send my beloved son; it may be they will respect him." But when the tenants saw him, they said to themselves, "This is the heir; let us kill him, that the inheritance may be ours." And they cast him out of the vineyard and killed him. What then will the owner of the vineyard do to them? He will come and destroy those tenants, and give the vineyard to others.'

(Luke 20:9–16a)

Of all the parables this is the one that seems to lend itself most readily to allegorical interpretation. For a start, the beloved son obviously refers to Jesus himself, and the expression seems to recall the words of Mark 1:11, 'Thou art my beloved Son'. It is only one step from there to the son's murder being a reference to the Cross. If Jesus is the son, must not the servants be the prophets of the Old Testament? Then Israel must be the vineyard and its leaders the tenants.

No wonder that Jülicher regarded this parable as an allegory and concluded that Jesus could not have told it; that it must be a creation of the early Church. No wonder either that quite a few critics have followed him.

The impression that this is an allegory is strengthened by the fact that the whole story seems so improbable: it looks rather like an artificial concoction in which every feature is meant to drive home a particular point but which, as a story, is really quite impossible.

That is precisely where the early critics were mistaken. It is now known that much of the land in Galilee belonged to absentee landlords, who cared little about the land and less their share of the produce. It is also known that the unrest in about the condition of their tenants, being only interested in the country, the revolutionary mood that in the end led to the Jewish War, had not only religious but also economic causes. The hostility to an absentee landlord portrayed in the parable was something that everyone listening to Jesus would be able to understand. Far from being far-fetched it was a feature from everyday life. So this story must certainly not be applied to God, who is not an absentee landlord.

But what did the tenants hope to gain by killing the son? The answer lies in the laws prevailing at the time. If a land-owner died without leaving an heir and without having made a will, his land was regarded as having no owner and could be claimed by any squatter. Possession being the better part of the law the tenants would be able to make out a good claim for themselves if their crime remained undiscovered.

The 'beloved son', far from being a re-echo of the voice at the Lord's baptism, is an indispensable feature of the story, for the expression is frequently used of an only son; and it is, of course, essential to the story that the son should be an only son.

Finally, the murder of the son is not a reference to the Cross. The Lord may have foreseen his death, but his listeners certainly did not. The murder is simply another feature of the story as a story.

With these things in mind, let us try to hear the story again. A landowner has a vineyard and lets it to tenants while he himself settles abroad. When the time comes he sends someone to collect the rent in kind, but he is given a hostile reception and no payment. When that happens several times, the landlord decides to send his son, hoping that this will bring the tenants to their senses. But when they see the son the tenants assume that the father must be dead and think that this is their chance to gain possession of the property. They kill him and deposit his body some distance away from the vineyard. The comment, 'They did not even give him a decent burial', so often made, is beside the point. Of course they did not: the body had to be found somewhere on the way to the vineyard but not too close by; it had to appear that he had been attacked and killed by a person or persons unknown.

A modern author could no doubt have written a very thrilling 'whodunnit' on how the culprits were brought to justice, but the parable is content to give only a conjectured outcome: the tenants would be found guilty and hanged.

What is the point of the parable? Once we realize that the listeners did not see, indeed, could not see, any specific significance in the various details, it is obvious that the point lies in the tenants' refusal to come to their senses, to take the last opportunity to pay up. And therefore they would have to pay the penalty.

The encounter with Jesus is the great opportunity. There have been opportunities before, but this one is critical, this one is final. Religious people are always talking about giving God his due. In concrete terms, giving God his due means accepting his Kingdom, that is to say, accepting Christ the King.

There has been an inclination to regard this parable as an allegory of God's patient dealing with his people in first sending the prophets and eventually the Son, and of the people's rejection of him culminating in the Cross. There are already indications of that in Mark's version, and they have become noticeably more pronounced in Luke and especially in Matthew. The son is thrown out of the vineyard, in Mark's Gospel after, in the others before he was killed. Killing him outside the vineyard could have been a natural feature of the story, part of the cover-up of the crime, but as Mark regards the vineyard as the scene of the murder it is probable that the later versions refer to the fact that Jesus was crucified outside the walls. Matthew also has two groups of servants, which may refer to the two groups of prophetic writings in the Old Testament.

Matthew and Luke also add the suggestion that the Kingdom of God will be taken away from Israel and given to another nation; in Luke this is merely a suggestion (v.16); in Matthew it is quite explicit (v.41).

The effect of this is that the parable loses its point, not only in relation to the first listeners but also in respect of any readers. The readers will get the comfortable feeling that Israel has lost its claim to the inheritance and that they have now entered into it. It would be interesting to know whether that is true. However, the New Testament offers ample evidence that it is not; or, at least, it is not the whole truth: God does not give up his claim on his people Israel, nor does he become unfaithful. In any case, do we really believe that the Lord told this parable merely to stroke the pious hairs of future Gentile Christians?

Today, as in the days when Jesus first told this parable, we are confronted with him. In him God claims us for himself. We can, if we like, put that in more precise terms. We owe it to God that we should accept Jesus Christ and believe in him, that we should follow and obey him. Those precise terms are not in the parable: they are an application, not an interpretation. But the interpretation that lies behind it is the same as it was at first. The encounter with Jesus is our great opportunity, the critical and final opportunity which decides our desiny.

The excuses

And again Jesus spoke to them in parables, saying,

'The kingdom of heaven may be compared to a king who gave a marriage feast for his son, and sent his servants to call those who were invited to the marriage feast; but they would not come. Again he sent other servants, saying, "Tell those who are invited, Behold, I have made ready my dinner, my oxen and my fat calves are killed, and everything is ready; come to the marriage feast." But they made

43

light of it and went off, one to his farm, another to his business, while the rest seized his servants, treated them shamefully, and killed them. The king was angry, and he sent his troops and destroyed those murderers and burned their city. Then he said to his servants, "The wedding is ready, but those invited were not worthy. Go therefore to the thoroughfares, and invite to the marriage feast as many as you find." And those servants went out into the streets and gathered all whom they found, both bad and good; so the wedding hall was filled with guests.' (Matthew 22:1–10)

When one of those who sat at table with him heard this, he said to him, 'Blessed is he who shall eat bread in the kingdom of God!' But he said to him,
'A man once gave a great banquet, and invited many; and at the time for the banquet he sent his servant to say to those who had been invited, "Come; for all is now ready." But they all alike began to make excuses. The first said to him, "I have bought a field, and I must go out and see it; I pray you, have me excused." And another said, "I have bought five yoke of oxen, and I go to examine them; I pray you, have me excused." And another said, "I have married a wife, and therefore I cannot come." So the servant came and reported this to his master. Then the householder in anger said to his servant, "Go out quickly to the streets and lanes of the city, and bring in the poor and maimed and blind and lame." And the servant said, "Sir, what you commanded has been done, and still there is room." And the master said to the servant, "Go out to the highways and hedges, and compel people to come in, that my house may be filled. For I tell you, none of those men who were invited shall taste my banquet." ' (Luke 14:15–24)

Matthew and Luke relate this parable in very different versions. It is therefore unlikely that it was contained in Q. The two evangelists must each have found it in a tradition that was unknown to the other.

The version in Matthew shows two features which cannot be original. The idea that the host, in this version a king, would send troops to destroy those who had refused to accept his invitation seems ludicrous. Moreover, by the time the soldiers had finished with the job the meal would have been spoiled. These verses are obviously not part of the parable as told at first; they are a clumsy intrusion into what was otherwise a perfectly good story. But it is not difficult to see why these verses were added. They refer to the destruction of Jerusalem in the Jewish War (70 AD). They are, however, completely out of character with the rest of the story.

The other feature which was not part of the original parable (following in vv.11–14) is the guest without festive clothes. This is really another parable, and we have therefore not included it here: it is discussed by itself (see pp. 97–99).

Luke's version too may contain an addition. There is no doubt that he regarded the two groups of new guests as references to two distinct groups of people: those from the streets and lanes of the city are the 'publicans and sinners' of Israel who take the place of the Pharisees and other godly people; those from the highways and hedges are the Gentiles. That was certainly not what the Lord had in mind. But it does not necessarily follow that the second attempt to fill the house was added by Luke or his source. Jesus may well have included this feature himself to emphasize the host's determination to make his house full.

Luke also provides a context for the parable. Of course, there is no absolute certainty that this is the context in which the parable was actually told, but he cannot have been far wrong: the story demands this kind of situation.

Jesus is at a meal in the house of a Pharisee. As one might expect in that kind of company, the conversation turns to the Kingdom of God, and one of the guests exclaims, 'Blessed is he who shall eat bread in the kingdom of God!' One often meets people like that, who have the right kind of devotional exclamation ready for all occasions!

Three things are tacitly implied in this exclamation. First of all that the Kingdom of God is something festive, something enjoyable. The rabbis often referred to the Kingdom as a banquet. They were speaking figuratively, of course, but the expectation of great joy was not meant figuratively, it was meant in a very literal sense, and rightly so.

Secondly, it never occurs to this man that he might not take part in God's eternal joy.

And thirdly, the Kingdom of God is here regarded as something far in the future. Actually, it was rabbinic teaching that the Kingdom of God is not merely something in the future. God is King now. He demands our obedience now. Every Jew was under the Law of God the King, and a proselyte, a Gentile who became a Jew by circumcision, 'took on the yoke of the Kingdom of God'. All the same, it was obvious that God did not receive universal obedience. They therefore looked forward to the time when God would be seen to be King, to that eternal realm of peace and righteousness in which there would be no room for sin.

The trouble with such looking forward is that it can so easily paralyse our attempts to do what God requires now. Both the rabbis and later Christian preachers have tried to warn against that danger by pointing out that the question when the Last Day will be is irrelevant inasmuch as our own Last Day will be the day we die—and as no one knows when he is going to die, we should live every day as if it were our last.

However, that is not quite the point the parable makes. Let us first look at the story. A man has arranged a big party and has invited a large number of guests. As was the custom, they have first had a general invitation, which they have accepted, and now they receive a last minute reminder. But suddenly they have other things to do. Some of the excuses are so transparent as to become insulting. Looking over a piece of land when you have already bought it? Inspecting ten head of cattle after you have already paid your money? But maybe they just wanted the host to beg them to put off their engagements, and intended to go to the feast all along.

The point is clear. Here are these religious people in Israel. They are forever talking about the Kingdom of God. Now is the moment to recognize the King, to give him their faith and their obedience. For the Kingdom of God is right in their midst. Christ the King is sitting there, right at their table. The blessedness of the Kingdom is theirs for the taking, now.

The Evangelists were right in seeing that the parable referred directly to the people who heard it. The encounter with Christ is the invitation to the Kingdom—and if they will not accept, the invitation will go to others.

But the invitation has not become past tense. It is true, of course, that his own people did not receive Jesus, and that others did receive him and thereby were made God's people.

But the invitation still stood when the Gospels were written, and it still stands today. The encounter with Jesus still is the hour of crisis, the moment of decision. The parable is not meant for people to say, 'Well said.' It is meant to draw attention to the fact that the King is here and demands faith and obedience, now.

Of course, there are side-issues. The Pharisee who made the exclamation is reminiscent of those people who are for ever saying that there is so much that is wrong in the world, and therefore speak in the most glowing terms of the Lord's second coming when all will change—but who make no attempt to change the world now. Granted, we shall not bring about the Kingdom of God. But there are things that can be done now, there are changes that can be brought about now. There is an obedience which the King demands now . . . And there is also a joy which the King will give now.

The guests in the parable remind us of that fatal inclination, which so many of us have, to neglect the things we ought to be doing because we have other things on our minds or on our hands. It is amazing how good we are at finding excuses why we should not do uncongenial jobs: we always have something else to do. It is even more amazing how we manage to lose the joys which God wants us to have, because we are so busy. We are so busy doing things which we could easily put off till tomorrow that we have no time to do the things which we ought to do today or to enjoy the experiences which we might have today. The New Testament is very insistent about the *kairos*, a word that cannot easily be translated into English, which refers to the right moment, the precise moment when a thing ought to be done, to the opportunity that must be grasped today, for tomorrow will be too late. It is no good doing tomorrow what Christ wants us to do today. And, whilst we should not put off till tomorrow what should be done today, we should not do today what could profitably be put off till tomorrow. Know the *kairos*, know the right moment. Know what the King wants us to do today.

However, that is not just a general comment. It is an important truth which we should act on because the living Lord is here. Meeting Christ is the hour of crisis, the moment of decision. The King demands our faith and obedience now.

The playing children

'But to what shall I compare this generation? It is like children sitting in the market places and calling to their playmates,
    "We piped to you, and you did not dance;
    we wailed and you did not mourn."
For John came neither eating nor drinking, and they say, "He has a demon"; the Son of man came eating and drinking, and they say, "Behold, a glutton and a drunkard, a friend of tax collectors and sinners!" Yet wisdom is justified by her deeds.'

(Matthew 11 : 16–9)

'To what then shall I compare the men of this generation, and what are they like? They are like children sitting in the market place and calling to one another,
    "We piped to you, and you did not dance;
    we wailed, and you did not weep."
For John the Baptist has come eating no bread and drinking no wine; and you say, "He has a demon." The Son of man has come eating and drinking; and you say, "Behold, a glutton and a drunkard, a friend of tax collectors and sinners!" Yet wisdom is justified by all her children.'

(Luke 7 : 31–5)

This parable is not, like so many, a story, but a straight comparison, and in this case the application forms an essential part of it. This application cannot have been added by the early Church. However important the ministry of John was in the tradition of the early Church, there was no doubt in the minds of early Christians that there was a world of difference between John and the Lord, difference not only in appearance, in lifestyle and in their work but of a much more fundamental nature, and it would have been impossible for them to put them side by side in the way the application of this parable does.

We have here therefore one of the very few examples of the Lord's own application of a parable, and it should be noted at once, that it is specific: it refers to a particular situation. True, as we shall see, it will also allow of a more general application, but that is not the point. The Lord himself used it specifically with reference to people's reaction to his own ministry and that of John the Baptist.

The parable itself is simple enough, a picture of children in the village square. Some of them want to play, and some boys suggest, 'Let us play at weddings,' but their playmates say, 'Oh no, not that.' Then a few girls suggest, 'Well then, let us play at funerals,' but the reaction is the same, and so a quarrel starts. The quarrel seems to be about what they are going to play, but the plain truth is that some do not want to play at all. It is a scene that one can observe only too often. Some children want to play, and they will fall in with anything that is suggested, but others are just out to spoil the pleasure of their friends.

That is exactly the way in which many people react to the ministry of Christ, and the way in which they have reacted to the ministry of John. John was a stern man who confronted people with God's judgment on their lives, not only by what he said but also by the way he lived. There was something puritanical about him. The seriousness of the situation and the sternness of his message did not allow for any luxurious living; so there he was, dressed in a hairy shirt, eating the cheapest food he could find and abstaining from alcohol, calling the nation to humble itself before God the Judge. And the reaction? 'This man is a fanatic. He is mad. We cannot listen to him!'

Then Jesus came. He too knew of God's judgment, but his first concern was to bring forgiveness. Through him God extended the hand of friendship to the sinners and accepted them into his fellowship, made them part of the family of God. He confronted people with God's generosity. And he too did not only preach about such things: he lived by that generosity. He therefore accepted the good things of life. The soldiers who crucified him were to comment on the quality of his clothes (John 19:23–4; but it may also be implied in Mark 15:24 and parallels). His ministry entailed considerable hardships, but he did not seek those hardships for their own sakes. He seems to have liked his food and to have appreciated a good wine. It is suggested in several places that, whenever there was something to celebrate, Jesus was the life and soul of the party.

49

One might be inclined to think that those who had criticized John for being too severe would now flock to Jesus; but not so. On the contrary, the same people who had condemned John for being too stern did not want to have anything to do with Jesus because he was too mild: 'Look at that man. Calls himself a prophet! He is just a glutton and a drunkard. And the company he keeps: a friend of tax collectors and other bad characters!'

In a sense this is another parable of excuses (cf. pp. 43–48). However, these excuses seem to go deeper: they concern the Lord himself, his message and his person. There is an apparent seriousness about the decision. Both John and Jesus are rejected because of what they say, and what they do. But if in fact John was rejected because he was not like Jesus and Jesus was rejected because he was not like John, then people would have made a choice between them. Instead, it was the same people who had rejected John who also rejected Christ; and some of the Lord's most faithful disciples had originally been disciples of John. The plain fact is that many people did not wish to be confronted with God's truth in whatever way it was presented.

The parable and its application are, of course, not a mere statement of fact. They are designed to pull up the listeners: do not be like those children. It may be right, indeed necessary, to become child-like; there is no need to be childish. Recognize the work that God was doing in John. Recognize God at work in Me. Follow me and play God's game.

The final phrase is not quite clear. It has been handed down in two versions. They are probably translations of the same Aramaic phrase, but we cannot tell whether Matthew or Luke has translated correctly. If Matthew was right, the Lord meant that the outcome will show how right it was for God in his wisdom first to send John and then Jesus; if Luke was right, the Lord wanted to convey that the 'children of wisdom', that is to say the wise, will recognize God's wisdom in sending both John and himself.

In either case, however, he leaves no doubt that John and he himself belong together, that they were both sent by divine wisdom, that they are both part of God's plan. The refusal to follow firstly, John the Baptist, then Jesus, is a refusal to be confronted with the living God. Do not refuse to see God when he visits you.

Though spoken in a specific context, this parable seems to lend itself to a wider application. It is a very widespread experience that people still react in the same way to the proclamation of the Gospel. Rejection of the Gospel often hides behind criticism of those who preach it or of 'the Christians' in general. One parson is too high, the other too low, one is too stern, the other too mild, one is too narrow, the other too liberal, one keeps himself too much to himself, the other hobnobs about with the riff-raff; one Christian is too serious, the other is too cheerful, one is too strict, the other takes life too easy, one is a do-gooder who always wants to improve people's lot, the other does not care enough about people. You just cannot win.

It can be a great comfort to Christians, and to Christian workers in particular, that in this respect they share what the Lord himself experienced. The servant can expect no better reception than his Lord. He will just have to live his Christian life and carry on his Christian work in the way he understands it. It would be futile to change either our words or our actions to counter all criticism. If one excuse is no longer valid, another is sure to be found.

However, that is true only inasmuch as we are indeed following Christ. We must reject the common fallacy that we must be right if everybody believes us, but we must also guard against the even more pernicious error that we could only be right if everybody contradicts us. The criterion lies in Christ.

We are thus brought back to the parable as first told by him. This, he says, is how people reacted to John and how they react to Me. Now what is your reaction?

The unjust steward

He also said to the disciples,
'There was a rich man who had a steward, and charges were brought to him that this man was wasting his goods. And he called

51

him and said to him, "What is this that I hear about you? Turn in the account of your stewardship, for you can no longer be steward." And the steward said to himself, "What shall I do, since my master is taking the stewardship away from me? I am not strong enough to dig, and I am ashamed to beg. I have decided what to do, so that people may receive me into their houses when I am put out of the stewardship." So, summoning his master's debtors one by one, he said to the first, "How much do you owe my master?" He said, "A hundred measures of oil." And he said to him, "Take your bill and sit down quickly and write fifty." Then he said to another, "And how much do you owe?" He said, "A hundred measures of wheat." He said to him, "Take your bill and write eighty." The master commended the dishonest steward for his prudence; for the sons of this world are wiser in their own generation than the sons of light.'

(Luke 16:1–8)

This parable is accompanied by a number of different applications which, as Dodd has observed, give the impression of being notes for a number of sermons on the story. However, it is advisable to look at the parable without those applications. Unfortunately, we do not know whether the parable ends at v.8 or 7; in other words, whether it was the steward's master who commended the dishonest steward, or whether it was Jesus. The RSV chooses the first of these possibilities.

It has, however, been more usual to take the other line. Is it likely that the master, who was, after all, the victim of the fraud, would commend the dishonest steward? Strange though it may seem, that is indeed possible. Really, it all depends on why the steward is called dishonest. Is it because of his conduct before or after he had heard that he was to be dismissed?

There is in the parable no suggestion that he was dismissed for dishonesty, merely for incompetence. But there might have been another kind of dishonesty involved. The Law forbade the taking of interest. However, the Scribes realized that the Law aimed at preventing the exploitation of the poor and was never intended to stop business transactions. It was therefore interpreted as applying only if the borrower did not himself possess the commodity he wanted to borrow. If therefore a poor man really had no money at all and he wanted to borrow some, no interest could be charged. But if a businessman wanted to borrow money or if he wanted to buy, say, wheat on credit, he would have to pay interest.

In time, however, the interpretation acquired the same authority as the Law. The result was that, whether the borrower was rich or poor, if he had already some of the commodity he wanted to borrow, he had to pay interest. As everybody, however poor, was likely to have at least some wheat and some oil in the house, these two things in particular were rarely lent without interest.

The way in which this was done was simply that the borrower signed a note in which he promised to pay back more than he borrowed. He might borrow one measure of oil and promise to pay back two, or he might borrow four measures of wheat and promise to pay back five. The parable suggests business transactions rather than private borrowing, and the debtors would have bought fifty measures of oil and eighty measures of wheat on credit, promising to pay for one hundred measures each.

According to the Scribes that was all perfectly in order and above board, but ordinary folk had the feeling that this was just a clever way of circumventing the Law. It was, in fact, evidence of the working of a legalistic mind that is always trying to think out how much one can get away with without actually breaking the Law. The Law, in this case, is God's law; and it is possible to observe meticulously the letter of the law, without asking, what does God really want us to do? It is also possible to interpret the law in such a way that its real intentions are not realized. In both cases the letter of the law becomes a pretext for disobeying God.

If that is what the Lord had in mind, the story is quite straightforward. Faced with a sudden crisis the steward decided to make himself friends by annulling the dishonest contracts and substituting honest ones. When his master found out, there was not much he could do about it, and he decided to make the best of the situation: by approving the steward's conduct he could take some of the credit himself.

If we interpret the parable in this way, it could be regarded as an attack on the legalistic attitude of the Scribes who use the letter of the Law to evade God's will. If people like the steward and his master realize at a time of crisis that their best interests are served by keeping on the right side of the Law and of their neighbours, how much more ought godly people to realize that it is profitable to keep on the right side of God and his will.

But is that really what the Lord wanted to convey? Is not the point of the parable that the steward, at a moment of crisis, took appropriate action? The trouble with so many religious people is that they waffle but do not act. They admire Jesus but do not follow him. They talk about the Kingdom of God but do not serve the King. People are not usually so careless about their secular affairs. They know what to do in a crisis. They ought to know what to do when they are confronted with Christ.

The approach to the judge

'Make friends quickly with your accuser, while you are going with him to court, lest your accuser hand you over to the judge, and the judge to the guard, and you be put in prison; truly, I say to you, you will never get out till you have paid the last penny.'

(Matthew 5:25–6)

'And why do you not judge for yourselves what is right? As you go with your accuser before the magistrate, make an effort to settle with him on the way, lest he drag you to the judge, and the judge hand you over to the officer, and the officer put you in prison. I tell you, you will never get out till you have paid the very last copper.'

(Luke 12:57–9)

Matthew and Luke have this saying in entirely different contexts. In Matthew it is part of the Lord's teaching about people making peace with one another. It is closely linked with his warning that making peace with your neighbour is more important even than making a sacrifice on the altar (5:23–4).

Important teaching indeed! But we feel that Luke was right when he put this saying side by side with the parable of the Way the Wind blows (12:54–6; see page 36). That parable emphasized the need to recognize the signs of the time: when meeting Jesus people should perceive that the Kingdom of God has come close by.

This parable is not a true parallel. It takes the argument one step further. If it is true that the Kingdom of God has come close by, then this is the hour of crisis. Usually people know what to do in an hour of crisis. They know that it is sensible to settle a case out of court, if possible. They may sometimes let matters drag on too long, but if they have any sense they will settle even at the last moment. The encounter with Jesus is just such a crisis and needs immediate action before it is too late.

4

The Great Chance

THE confrontation with Christ is the hour of crisis. But that also means that it is the moment of opportunity. It would be a great mistake to think that we are merely called to avoid God's judgment. The Christian faith is no such negative thing. It is, in fact, the most positive thing possible. Christ offers the most intimate relationship with God and thereby a fullness of life that cannot be experienced in any other way.

The treasure in the field and the pearl of great value

'The kingdom of heaven is like treasure hidden in a field, which a man found and covered up; then in his joy he goes and sells all that he has and buys that field.

Again, the kingdom of heaven is like a merchant in search of fine pearls, who, on finding one pearl of great value, went and sold all that he had and bought it.'

(Matthew 13:44-6)

These two parables are related by Matthew as a pair, and it is possible that they were told by Jesus one after the other. The first parable is about a man who finds treasure in a field. In times of war especially valuables are often buried, and if the owner dies before he has recovered his property it will remain buried until it is found by chance. The man who finds it is evidently not a wealthy man: he has to sell all that he has in order to buy the piece of land. The morality of his action is not questioned. The characters in our Lord's stories do not

57

always act according to the strictest morality: they are just people like one might find anywhere, and they act as people often do act. The point is that this man has found something that is worth giving everything up for, and he acts accordingly. He sells all that he has so that he can lay his hands on something worth much more. Such a find is the encounter with Jesus. Knowing him and following him is worth the sacrifice of all else.

The man in the second parable is a wealthy jeweller, who finds a pearl of extraordinary value. Wealthy though he is he has to sell all that he has in order to buy this one pearl. But he knows it is worth it. Here too the point is clear. The encounter with Jesus and the opportunity to follow him is worth more than all the treasures in the world.

The hour of crisis is here the great opportunity. This is the one big chance these men had. They had to act at once, before someone else discovered the treasure and bought the land, before someone else made a better offer for the pearl. But to take advantage of this opportunity these men had to take a chance: they had to risk all that they had, trusting that their new treasure would prove worth the price. That is what the encounter with Christ is like. It demands quick thinking; one cannot put off the decision. It demands putting all other considerations to one side and giving all else up. It demands taking a chance on Jesus and therefore the confidence that he is worth taking a chance on.

He is worth it. But we can find that out only in the act of faith itself, in actually following him.

The talents and the pounds

'For it will be as when a man going on a journey called his servants and entrusted to them his property; to one he gave five talents, to another two, to another one, to each according to his ability. Then he went away. He who had received the five talents went at once and traded with them; and he made five talents more. So also, he who had the two talents made two talents more. But he who had received the one talent, went and dug in the ground and hid his master's money. Now afer a long time the master of those servants came and settled accounts with them. And he who had received the five talents *came forward, bringing five talents more, saying, "Master, you delivered to me five talents; here I have made five talents more." His master said to him, "Well done, good and faithful servant; you have been faithful over a little, I will set you over much; enter into the joy of your master." And he also who had the two talents came forward, saying, "Master, you delivered to me two talents; here I have made two talents more." His master said to him, "Well done, good and faithful servant; you have been faithful over a little, I will set you over much; enter into the joy of your master." He also who had received the one talent came forward, saying, "Master, I knew you to be a hard man, reaping where you did not sow, and gathering where you did not winnow; so I was afraid, and I went and hid your talent in the ground. Here you have what is yours." But his master answered him, "You wicked and slothful servant! You knew that I reap where I have not sowed, and gather where I have not winnowed? Then you ought to have invested my money with the bankers, and at my coming I should have received what was my own with interest. So take the talent from him, and give it to him who has the ten talents. For to every one who has will more be given, and he will have abundance; but from him who has not, even what he has will be taken away. And cast the worthless servant into the outer darkness; there men will weep and gnash their teeth." '*

(Matthew 25:14–30)

As they heard these things, he proceeded to tell a parable, because he was near to Jerusalem, and because they supposed that the kingdom of God was to appear immediately. He said therefore,

'A nobleman went into a far country to receive kingly power and then return. Calling ten of his servants, he gave them ten pounds, and said to them, "Trade with these till I come." But his citizens hated him and sent an embassy after him, saying, "We do not want this man to reign over us." When he returned, having received the kingly power, he commanded these servants, to whom he had given the money, to be called to him, that he might know what they had gained by trading. The first came before him, saying, "Lord, your pound has made ten pounds more." And he said to him, "Well done, good servant! Because you have been faithful in a very little, you shall have authority over ten cities." And the second came, saying, "Lord, your pound made five pounds." And he said to him, "And you are to be over five cities." Then another came, saying, "Lord, here is your pound, which I kept laid away in a napkin; for I was afraid of you, because you are a severe man; you take up what you did not lay down, and reap what you did not sow." He said to him, "I will condemn you out of your own mouth, you wicked servant! You knew that I was a severe man, taking up what I did not lay down and reaping what I did not sow? Why then did you not put my money into the bank, and at my coming I should have collected it

with interest?" And he said to those who stood by, "Take the pound from him and give it to him who has the ten pounds." (And they said to him, "Lord, he has ten pounds!") "I tell you, that to every one who has will more be given; but from him who has not, even what he has will be taken away. But as for these enemies of mine, who did not want me to reign over them, bring them here and slay them before me."

(Luke 19:11–27)

When we read this parable it is extremely difficult to dissociate it from its traditional interpretation. That is true particularly of the form in which Matthew has it. To us a talent means a natural gift, an ability to do certain things. Of course, we can see that in the parable it is a sum of money, and we may even know that our use of the word talent comes from an interpretation of the parable, but it does not easily occur to us that 'talent' as we understand it might come from a mistaken interpretation of the parable. We therefore take it for granted that talent = a sum of money stands for talent = natural endowment.

The parable then is often believed to mean this. We have all received certain gifts. These gifts are from God, and we are responsible for the way in which we use them. As we have not all received the same gifts—some are more gifted, more talented, than others—we will be judged accordingly. Those to whom much has been given, of them will much be required. But even if our talents are limited, that is no excuse for not using them.

That is all very true, but is it really what this parable is about?

To answer that question with complete confidence we really ought to know exactly how and when it was told, and to whom. Unfortunately we do not know. This parable has been handed down in two very different versions. Though we cannot dismiss altogether the possibility that the Lord may have told it more than once, it still remains true that it is the same parable in two versions. Moreover, as in Luke's version it is clearly mixed up with another story, and we can take it for granted that Jesus himself knew what he was talking about, we must look for one salient point which both versions have in common.

One thing is certain. The master in the parable does not
stand for God. It would be blasphemous to suggest that God
'reaps where he did not sow'!

It is also obvious that the nobleman going to a foreign
country to receive kingly power does not belong to the parable.
It is a story by itself that takes its cue from the fact that the
petty princelings of Herod's dynasty on their accession to the
throne had to receive confirmation of their claims from the
Roman Senate. We can no longer say with certainty why Jesus
told the story, but the phrase, 'We do not want this man to
reign over us', may refer to the Lord's rejection by the nation.
Luke, in inserting it here seems to have thought specifically of
the Lord's trial before Pilate.

We should also note that the difference in the sums of money
entrusted to the servants, which seems such a prominent feature
of Matthew's version, and which has inspired the traditional
interpretation of the talents as varying natural endowments, is
absent from Luke's version. On the other hand, in Luke's
version, where all the servants receive the same amount of
money, they vary in the amount of profit they make.

The one feature that the two versions have in common is
that the 'unfaithful' servant is afraid, that is to say, he did not
dare to take any risks. It is all very well to be wise after the
event, but the servants who did use the money could also have
been less fortunate and lost it all. What would the master
have said if they had had to tell him, 'We traded with your
money, and we lost it all!'? The same is true of the bank.
Banks are not always safe: they have been known to go bank-
rupt. Better to play safe. It may not produce any profit, but at
least the money is safe.

If what we have said so far is right, the parable refers to the
risk one has to take in following Jesus. Following him meant
taking him on trust. It also meant, leaving the well-established
paths of traditional piety and starting on a road leading one
knew not where.

The Lord's own life was a life of taking risks. The criticism
levelled against him by his opponents was that he did not lead
the kind of circumspect life that one might expect of a rabbi.
By seeking the company of low characters and being a friend

of moral and religious outcasts he not only set a bad example but also endangered his own moral standards. Bad company ruins good morals.

There was also another kind of risk he took. Somehow we cannot think of our Lord as living dangerously. Yet the outcome shows that is exactly what he did. Of all the really great teachers of mankind he is the only one whose ministry ended in disaster so soon.

However, he was not speaking about his own risk. He was pointing out that, just as in our secular lives, if we want to succeed, we must take chances, so, if we want to meet God's demands, we must take our chance on him. That was needed at the time when he first told the parable; it is still needed today.

Of course, the direct application is not always the same. The first disciples, when confronted with the Lord's call, had to make a choice between the safe ways of traditional religion and this Man Jesus. They had nothing to go by, other than the fact that they found him someone worthy of their trust: he himself was the only guide they had. So they had to take him on trust; they had to take a chance on him.

Centuries later Blaise Pascal was to speak of faith as a wager or a bet on God. He lived at a time when there was a great interest in the philosophical approach to religion, but he had discovered that all speculation about God is in vain. What we need is not the god of the philosophers but the God of Abraham, Isaac and Jacob, the God and Father of our Lord Jesus Christ. That means putting our trust in Christ. But only if we actually do that, if we actually take that risk, will we find out we have backed a winner.

Today the situation is different again. The climate of our age is agnostic. The phenomenal world is the world we know. If there is a God we know nothing about him, and it seems safer to build our lives on what we know rather than on speculations about a God who may or who may not 'exist'. In any case, as there are so many religions, which do you choose?

There is no theoretical answer to that question. If we make a choice it has to be made on trust. That may seem a rather haphazard way of going about it, but then many of our most important decisions have to be made that way. Thus, for example, it has been said that marriage is a lottery. True, marriage means that two people have to take each other on trust, and we all know that in some cases it does not work out—though we must not forget that in many cases it does! At any rate, we can only find out what marriage is like by taking each other on trust and being married.

In fact, many ordinary things in life can only be found out in action, we can only learn about them by doing them. Whatever the value of sex-instruction, we can only learn what it is to love and be loved by actually engaging it in. However attractive the illustrations in some of those modern cookery books, the proof of the pudding is still in the eating. However much we may like to look at travel brochures, we never come to know a country until we actually visit it.

And we will never come to know God unless we actually follow Christ. That is the chance we must take. It is, indeed, a leap in the dark. But only when we do take it will we discover that we land in God, the liivng God.

5

God is Not To Be Mocked

THE encounter with Christ is the great opportunity. But the crisis which he brings is a serious one, the decisions which we take now will stand, and we are under God's judgment. God should not be mocked by making light of his judgment.

Dives and Lazarus

'There was a rich man, who was clothed in purple and fine linen and who feasted sumptuously every day. And at his gate lay a poor man named Lazarus, full of sores, who desired to be fed with what fell from the rich man's table; moreover the dogs came and licked his sores. The poor man died and was carried by the angels to Abraham's bosom. The rich man also died and was buried; and in Hades, being in torment, he lifted up his eyes, and saw Abraham far off and Lazarus in his bosom. And he called out, "Father Abraham, have mercy upon me, and send Lazarus to dip the end of his finger in water and cool my tongue; for I am in anguish in this flame." But Abraham said, "Son, remember that you in your lifetime received your good things, and Lazarus in like manner evil things; but now he is comforted here, and you are in anguish. And besides all this, between us and you a great chasm has been fixed, in order that those who would pass from here to you may not be able, and none may cross from there to us." And he said, "Then I beg you, father, to send him to my father's house, for I have five brothers, so that he may warn them, lest they also come into this place of torment." But Abraham said, "They have Moses and the prophets; let them hear them." And he said, "No, father Abraham; but if some one goes to them from the dead, they will repent." He said to him, "If they do not hear Moses and the prophets, neither will they be convinced if some one should rise from the dead." '

(Luke 16: 19–31)

65

The Kingdom of God is Like This

As far as we know this is the only parable for which Jesus borrowed the story. The story circulated in Egypt many centuries before Christ and was probably brought to Palestine by Alexandrian Jews. Being a borrowed story, it cannot be taken for granted that every detail reflects the Lord's own teaching. If we want to understand what the Lord wanted to convey, we shall have to look at where the parable differs from the traditional story, that is to say, the conversation beween Dives (the rich man) and Abraham.

In its earlier versions the story just relates a dramatic reversal of conditions between this life and the next. The rich man finds that he has had his pleasures and that now he must pay for them; the poor beggar receives the pleasures which he had never known while he was on earth.

In its Jewish form the story was adapted to popular beliefs about the after-life. The Pharisees believed that there was to be a resurrection of the dead at the end of the present age. God would raise the dead, and then the Last Judgment would take place. But what about the time between death and resurrection? Ancient Jewish belief held that the dead were in Sheol, and it would be obvious to believe that they would be kept there until the resurrection. Their condition in Sheol was not a kind of continued life; on the contrary, the characteristic thing about those in Sheol was precisely that they were life-less, though not extinct. But gradually there had arisen a belief that there were two groups awaiting the resurrection. The righteous were in Paradise, waiting to be raised to eternal life, and the wicked were in Hades = Sheol, awaiting their final condemnation, and both were conscious of their condition.

The Lord, when using the story as a parable, has left these features as he found them, without any comment. They are not his own teaching; in fact, as far as we know, he never gave any specific teaching on the subject. He did not, apparently, want to supply irrelevant information and answer unprofitable questions—he called people to make a decision.

The story as told by Jesus depicts the rich man just the way people are. He is wealthy, he has no care in the world, he does not have to work for a living, and he can spend his life as one big party. He is not depicted as particularly wicked, not even as less charitable than most folk: after all, he does not chase the beggar from his door, as some others might have done. But neither does he particularly care about him. There have always been rich and poor people in the world, God made them so, and it is no matter of concern to him.

No, Dives is not particularly wicked. Neither are we told that Lazarus is a particularly godly man. He is just poor and wretched, too wretched to be able to take responsible moral decisions: he is far too busy trying to beg a few scraps to feed himself and to keep the dirty alley dogs at a distance—without much success.

The trouble with Dives is that he does not really see Lazarus and his needs. Oh, yes, he does see him in a way: he even knows his name (v.24). But he does not really see him as a person, as an individual needing help, as someone who concerns him. And he does not regard his wealth as an opportunity to do something about his neighbour's need.

The Lord is thoroughly realistic about that. He knows that Dives cannot bear the load of the whole world on his shoulders and cannot put the whole world right. There is much in the Bible about social justice, and we can take it for granted that the notion of a just society was never far from the Lord's mind. The Kingdom of God has obvious connexions with the just society. But no one should wait for that Kingdom without obeying the King now. Dives lives in the world as it is now, a world in which he has everything and Lazarus has nothing. His having everything is an opportunity, an opportunity not merely to enjoy himself, not even merely to 'do good', but an opportunity to see Lazarus as someone who concerns him and to act accordingly.

There can be little doubt that this is one point that the Lord wanted to make. There is a second point in the passage which he added to the story, but this second point depends on the first and must not be isolated. The well-known story, Jesus wants to say, shows that the decisions are made in this life. The opportunity is now: when we are dead it will be too late.

In the additional part, the conversation between Dives and

Abraham, everything remains within the context of the story—
as we might expect in a parable. The rich man in his new condition remains himself. He takes it for granted that people like
Lazarus are still at his beck and call. He first expects him to be
available to give him some relief in his torment, and is probably
very surprised that it cannot be done. But surely, if Lazarus
cannot help him, he can at least be sent to help his five brothers.
The miracle of his return from the dead and his first-hand
knowledge of conditions beyond the grave will persuade his
brothers that it is necessary to change their lives!

The answer is the point of this added part. Both he and his
brothers have received all the knowledge they needed. They
have Moses and the Prophets. God has spoken through Moses
and the Prophets, and his Word should be enough. If people
are not persuaded by what God has said, they will not be convinced by any miracle.

At this point we ought to ask the question: to whom was
Jesus speaking? It is sometimes suggested that this parable was
aimed specifically at the Sadducees, who believed that there was
no resurrection and no judgment. The argument would then be,
even if they did not know of the coming judgment, they still
knew what God required of them. Even without hope of reward
or fear of condemnation God's people are expected to carry out
his will.

But can we be so certain? It must be doubted if the parable
would have that convincing power for anyone who would
regard the whole of the story as fantastic. To be sure, God's
will is valid regardless of any reward or punishment. But it
seems that the story would be much more convincing to someone who did expect the resurrection.

However, in either case the point remains the same. The
critical decision about life or death, eternal life or death, is
made in the encounter with God's word. God expects to be
taken at his word. He does not have to authenticate himself
by miracles. More precisely, Jesus does not have to prove that
God acts and speaks through him. He does not have to
authenticate himself. The encounter with him is enough. This
encounter is the moment of decision, the moment of crisis.

Jesus here pinpoints the message of the first part. Eternal things are decided in this life: the present life is the time of opportunity. The encounter with Jesus is the opportunity to hear the voice of God; it is also the opportunity to see the neighbour. These are not two different things. The knowledge of God makes it possible really to see the neighbour.

That is the great opportunity. It is also a great responsibility. God is not to be mocked. Refusing or failing to grasp the opportunity has the most serious consequences. No matter if we say, with Dives, that we did not know the consequences. That is no excuse. For we were given the opportunity.

The rich fool

> One of the multitude said to him, 'Teacher, bid my brother divide the inheritance with me.'
> But he said to him, 'Man, who made me a judge or divider over you?'
> And he said to them, 'Take heed, and beware of all covetousness; for a man's life does not consist in the abundance of his possessions.
> And he told them a parable, saying,
> 'The land of a rich man brought forth plentifully; and he thought to himself, "What shall I do, for I have nowhere to store my crops?" And he said, "I will do this: I will pull down my barns, and build larger ones; and there I will store all my grain and my goods. And I will say to my soul, Soul, you have ample goods laid up for many years; take your ease, eat, drink, be merry." But God said to him, "Fool! This night your soul is required of you; and the things you have prepared, whose will they be?" So is he who lays up treasure for himself, and is not rich toward God.'

(Luke 12:13–21)

Luke has handed this parable down in a particular context. There is, of course, no guarantee that it was actually told in reply to this request that Jesus should adjudicate in a quarrel about an inheritance, but even if Luke should be mistaken—which we cannot know—it is still true that some such situation was required, a situation in which the Lord wanted to warn someone of the danger of placing all his confidence in his possessions. It seems therefore advisable to interpret the parable in the context in which Luke has put it.

Rabbis were often asked to adjudicate in matters concerning property. There is therefore nothing out of the ordinary in the request. What is extraordinary is the Lord's refusal. It is not suggested anywhere in the New Testament that Jesus regarded wealth as such as a bad thing. That money is the root of all evil and that one should not contaminate oneself with it is a notion that was foreign to him. It is the attitude to money and the use that is made of it that makes it good or bad for us (cf. 1 Timothy 6:10; the love of money, that is to say, the greed for money is the root of all evils).

Neither does Jesus say that he will have nothing to do with 'worldly' things. On the contrary, the parable indicates that a man's wealth comes from God and therefore what he does with it is God's concern. But he does not wish to adjudicate this case because he sees the peril of covetousness, of greed (v.15).

The second part of v.15 can be interpreted in more than one way. The RSV translates, 'A man's life does not consist in the abundance of his possessions'; in other words, there is more to life than wealth. The NEB renders, 'Even when a man has more than enough, his wealth does not give him life'; in other words, wealth is no cure for death. The Jerusalem Bible says, similarly, 'A man's life is not made secure by what he owns, even when he has more than he needs'. However, we feel that Moffatt's translation, though a little awkward, comes closer to the original intention: 'A man's life is not part of his possessions because he has ample wealth'; the idea being that, however much we may possess, life is not part of our property, it remains in God's hands. That, after all, is illustrated by the parable.

The parable plays on the word *psyche*, usually rendered, 'soul'. Indeed, in the Aramaic used by Jesus the words which appear in Greek as *zoe*, 'life', (v.15) and *psyche* (vv.19–20) may well have been the same word. Actually the translation 'soul' is an unfortunate one. The New Testament does not know the notion of a soul as distinct from the body. 'Soul' in the New Testament is rather that quality which distinguishes living beings from dead objects. 'I will say to my soul' therefore just means, 'I will say to myself', and the phrase, 'Your soul is required of you,' simply means, 'Your life is to be taken from you.' The folly of the rich fool is that he thinks that his life, his 'soul' is part of his property, that he can enjoy both his life and his property as he chooses. He is mistaken. His life is not his own. It is in God's hands. Now that it is taken away from him he loses his property as well.

It may seem at first sight that the parable lacks the sense of urgency of many of the others. There seems to be no reference to a moment of decision. However, the rich fool has taken a decision: the wrong decision. He, like the man who found a treasure in a field and like the merchant in precious stones (Matthew 13:44-6), has put all his eggs in one basket, but it is the wrong basket. He has not taken the most important factor into account, and has therefore made the wrong decision. His folly does not so much lie in the selfishness of his choice—take your ease, eat, drink, be merry—as in the expectation that he has a future at all. He does not know that the judgment is now, and that his wrong decision leaves him helpless at the moment of death.

Luke has added a passage about the folly of anxiety.

And he said to his disciples,
'Therefore I tell you, do not be anxious about your life, what you shall eat, nor about your body, what you shall put on. For life is more than food, and the body more than clothing. Consider the ravens: they neither sow nor reap, they have neither storehouse nor barn, and yet God feeds them. Of how much more value are you than the birds! And which of you by being anxious can add a cubit to his span of life? If then you are not able to do as small a thing as that, why are you anxious about the rest? Consider the lilies, how they grow; they neither toil nor spin; yet I tell you, even Solomon in all his glory was not arrayed like one of these. But if God so clothes the grass which is alive in the field today and tomorrow is thrown into the oven, how much more will he clothe you, O men of little faith? And do not seek what you are to eat and what you are to drink, nor be of anxious mind. For all the nations of the world seek these things; and your Father knows that you need them. Instead, seek his kingdom, and these things shall be yours as well.
'Fear not, little flock, for it is your Father's good pleasure to give you the kingdom. Sell your possessions, and give alms; provide yourselves with purses that do not grow old, with a treasure in the

heavens that does not fail, where no thief approaches and no moth destroys. For where your treasure is, there will your heart be also.'
                                    (Luke 12:22–33; cf. Matthew 6:25–33; 19–21)

Luke has seen, quite rightly, that there can be a connexion between greed and anxiety. The man who came to Jesus about the inheritance needs to be cured not only of his greed but also of his anxiety. The parable had demonstrated that the anxiety that comes from greed is of no avail. The rich fool was anxious about what to do with his wealth; he managed to cope with the problem, but in the end it did him no good.

However, there is also an anxiety that comes from need, not greed. The Lord has also spoken about that. The real cure for worry is putting first things first. If we put God's Kingdom first, everything else falls into place, and there is no room for worry.

The Kingdom of God means first and foremost that God is in command. That implies two things. As God is in command we can trust him to provide. And as God is in command, we do as he tells us.

Worry is absurd. It achieves nothing. It also implies that we do not really believe that God is our Father.

The connexion with the parable is obvious. The rich fool had not put the Kingdom of God first: he had put himself first. He had not trusted in God: he had trusted in his possessions.

Yet this connexion is not original. Ineed, these sayings, true though they are, tend to take away the keen sharpness of the parable. This rich man had made his decision, the wrong decision, and the end is death. The judgment is now, and to him it spells death.

The infertile fig tree

And he told this parable:
'A man had a fig tree planted in his vineyard; and he came seeking fruit on it and found none. And he said to the vinedresser, "Lo, these three years I have come seeking fruit on this fig tree, and I find none. Cut it down; why should it use up the ground?" And he answered him, "Let it alone, sir, this year also, till I dig about it

and put on manure. And if it bears fruit next year, well and good;
but if not, you can cut it down." '

(Luke 13 : 6–9)

The parable of the infertile fig tree is entirely self-contained and should therefore not be elaborated too precisely. It is tempting to suggest that the vineyard is Israel, the fig tree is Jerusalem, the three years are the time since John the Baptist started his ministry and that the vinedresser is Jesus who offers one more year of grace. But the story relates an entirely secular event. A man who plants a fig tree in a vineyard will want to see results. The vineyard is his living and he cannot afford to let part of the land be taken up by a fig tree unless he gets something out of it. Farmers are quite unsentimental about the use of their land. They may set part of their land aside for non-commercial purposes, but only if they receive something out of it.

The one point of comparison in the parable is at the end. The encounter with Jesus is the final chance. God is generous and patient, but he is not to be mocked.

6

The Divine Generosity

JESUS leaves no doubt that God's judgment is to be taken seriously. It would be easy to single out those parables and sayings of his which stress that, and to suggest that he was first and foremost a prophet of judgment. That, however, would be misleading. In the final resort God's judgment is governed by his generosity.

That generosity is demonstrated in a number of parables. Two of those warn the listeners off making premature judgments. The others go much further and show examples of gracious giving and forgiving which point to God's grace and generosity.

The tares and the drag-net

Another parable he put before them, saying,
'The kingdom of heaven may be compared to a man who sowed good seed in his field; but while men were sleeping, his enemy came and sowed weeds among the wheat, and went away. So when the plants came up and bore grain, then the weeds appeared also. And the servants of the householder came and said to him, "Sir, did you not sow good seed in your field? How then has it weeds?" He said to them, "An enemy has done this." The servants said to him, "Then do you want us to go and gather them?" But he said, "No; lest in gathering the weeds you root up the wheat along with them. Let both grow together until the harvest; and at harvest time I will tell the reapers, Gather the weeds first and bind them in bundles to be burned, but gather the wheat into my barn." '

(Matthew 13 : 24–30)

The Kingdom of God is Like This

Then he left the crowds and went into the house. And his disciples come to him, saying,
'Explain to us the parable of the weeds of the field.'
He answered,
'He who sows the good seed is the Son of man; the field is the world, and the good seed means the sons of the kingdom; the weeds are the sons of the evil one, and the enemy who sowed them is the devil; the harvest is the close of the age, and the reapers are angels. Just as the weeds are gathered and burned with fire, so will it be at the close of the age. The Son of man will send his angels, and they will gather out of his kingdom all causes of sin and all evildoers, and throw them into the furnace of fire; there men will weep and gnash their teeth. Then the righteous will shine like the sun in the kingdom of their Father. He who has ears, let him hear.'

(Matthew 13 : 36–43)

'Again, the kingdom of heaven is like a net which was thrown into the sea and gathered fish of every kind; when it was full, men drew it ashore and sat down and sorted the good into vessels but threw away the bad. So it will be at the close of the age. The angels will come out and separate the evil from the righteous, and throw them into the furnace of fire; there men will weep and gnash their teeth.'

(Matthew 13 : 47–50)

Though Matthew has separated the two parables it is obvious that he regarded them as a pair. The interpretations even contain the same warning (vv.41–2; 49–50).

At first sight the parable of the Tares or weeds seems perhaps a little far-fetched, but cases are actually known in which an unfriendly neighbour did precisely this: sow 'tares' among somebody's wheat. The 'tares' are probably darnel, a weed that resembles wheat. That is why the suggestion made by the servants, sensible though it seems, is not accepted. Much better to let them grow together and sort them out at harvest time.

Matthew has given this parable an allegorical interpretation. There can be no doubt that he was mistaken in that. But he has seen correctly that both this parable and that of the drag-net contain a reference to the Last Judgment. However, that is not where the main point lies.

The point of the parable lies rather in the words, 'Let both grow together until the harvest.' The world has always had people who insisted on the instant creation of a congregation of saints: separate the true believers from those who are merely hangers-on and thus bring about an instant Kingdom of God! That cry, which today can be regarded as the dividing line between the Church and the sects, was also the motto of some of the smaller Jewish sects in our Lord's days as well as the ideal of the Pharisees. We can safely disregard the possibility that the parable was first spoken to followers of one of the minor sects, and we must therefore conclude that it is at least possible that Jesus had the Pharisees in mind. But we cannot be certain. There may well have been some of his own disciples who had the same feeling: let us keep the band of disciples pure. The inference of the parable then becomes obvious. If it is impossible to distinguish clearly between darnel and wheat, it is much wiser to let them both grow together until the harvest. Similarly, as it is impossible for humans to judge, let us not try to draw distinctions between those who follow Christ. They may be a motley crowd, but who are we to judge?

The parable of the drag-net makes the same point. When you use a drag-net you have no control over what might be caught in it; you sort it out when you have hauled it in. Similarly, let us not try to sort out Christ's followers until God's time.

Dodd extends the meaning of the parable to the work that the disciples were doing. The fishers of men must be prepared to cast their net widely over the whole field of human society. That is true enough, and it could be argued that it follows from the Lord's own ministry. But it must be doubted if the parable was told with that in mind. The parable rather refers to the Lord's attitude of being a friend of tax-gatherers and other bad characters in contrast with those who insisted that the good must be segregated from the bad, the godly from the ungodly, the true believers from those who are just hangers-on, here and now.

The labourers in the vineyard

'For the kingdom of heaven is like a householder who went out early in the morning to hire labourers for his vineyard. After agreeing with the labourers for a denarius a day, he sent them into his vineyard. And going out about the third hour he saw others standing idle in the market place; and to them he said, "You go into the vineyard too, and whatever is right I will give you." So they went. Going

77

out again about the sixth hour and the ninth hour, he did the same.
And about the eleventh hour he went out and found others standing;
and he said to them, "Why do you stand here idle all day?" They
said to him, "Because no one has hired us." He said to them, "You
go into the vineyard too." And when evening came, the owner of the
vineyard said to his steward, "Call the labourers and pay them their
wages, beginning with the last, up to the first." And when those hired
about the eleventh hour came, each of them received a denarius.
Now when the first came, they thought they would receive more;
but each of them also received a denarius. And on receiving it they
grumbled at the householder, saying, "These last worked only one
hour, and you have made them equal to us who have borne the
burden of the day and the scorching heat." But he replied to one of
them, "Friend, I am doing you no wrong; did you not agree with me
for a denarius? Take what belongs to you, and go; I choose to give
to this last as I give to you. Am I not allowed to do what I choose
with what belongs to me? Or do you begrudge my generosity?" So
the last will be first, and the first last.'

(Matthew 20: 1–16)

This parable differs from most in that the conduct of the householder is out of the ordinary. Usually people in the parables
behave as people normally do: this man is an exception. Nevertheless the parable remains an ordinary story in which nothing
stands for anything else. If the householder's conduct is unusual
and unexpected, however, the men's reaction is certainly not.

The opening scene must have been a common enough thing.
A man wants some workmen to harvest his grapes, and he goes
to the market place to find some. A suitable wage is agreed
between him and his labourers. There is no suggestion that the
men were forced to accept what he was prepared to offer, and,
in spite of many commentators' confident assurance that one
denarius was a normal daily wage, the amount seems on the
generous side, considering the value of money at the time. At
any rate, that was the amount they agreed on, and the men
were obviously anxious to work for that.

Then, in the course of the day, the owner of the vineyard
goes to the market again and again, and every time he finds
more men there standing idle and prepared to work for whatever he is willing to give them. As obviously these are all newly
arrived, one is inclined to comment that they do not seem to
have been particularly keen to find work, or they would have

been there earlier. However, nothing is said about that. We are only told that, when asked if they will work in the vineyard for whatever the householder thinks fit to give them, they go.

One can imagine their surprise when, at the end of the day, they receive a whole denarius for very little work. One can also understand the protest of the men who had worked all day and received the same.

Yet, as the Lord points out, is their protest justified? They have not been underpaid. They have received what is their due. If the owner of the vineyard wants to be generous to the others, that is his affair: it is none of their business. Of course, it is an extraordinary way of going about his business. But it is his money and he can please himself.

The context (following 19:23–30) suggests that the Evangelist understood this parable as referring to the Last Judgment. The Last Judgment will be a matter not merely of divine justice but of divine generosity. Actually, to the Hebrew mind those two concepts are not so very far apart. The word that we usually translate by 'righteousness' signifies more than mere justice. Nowhere in the Old Testament is it ever used in connexion with punishment or retribution. As the same word was also one of the names by which God was worshipped at Jerusalem, there are many passages, especially in the Psalms, where we should not try to define it too precisely; but where it can be defined it often refers specifically to God's saving acts. However, it is also used of human actions. A righteous person is one whose conduct conforms to the nation's Covenant with God. That often means, specifically, to take care of those in need, to practice charity, to bestow alms. It has little to do with 'justice' in the narrow sense: giving everybody his due, reward to the deserving and punishment to the guilty, payment to the worker and nothing to him who has not worked. Righteousness as the Old Testament understands it is, indeed, very close to generosity.

Therefore the action of the householder, though unusual, would have been understandable to a Jewish audience, and probably also to Matthew's readers. But was Jesus referring specifically to God's generosity at the Last Judgement?

Probably not, though we cannot really be sure. The Lord had a reputation for extending a hand of friendship to all and sundry, to the deserving and the undeserving. In doing that he proclaimed—actions speak louder and more clearly than words—that God accepted them for his own. He proclaimed the divine righteousness, the divine generosity, not at some time in a remote future but right now.

No, of course, the householder does not 'stand for Jesus himself' or 'for God'. He is just an extraordinarily generous householder. But if such generosity can be found occasionally among humans, surely God's generosity must be far greater.

Matthew's application of the parable to the Last Judgment is to some extent justified. We will, indeed, find that God's righteousness is of incredible generosity. But, Jesus says, you do not have to wait till then to find out. He accepts you now—and you can draw the consequences now.

The pharisee and the publican

> He also told this parable to some who trusted in themselves that they were righteous and despised others:
> 'Two men went up into the temple to pray, one a Pharisee and the other a tax collector. The Pharisee stood and prayed thus with himself, "God, I thank thee that I am not like other men, extortioners, unjust, adulterers, or even like this tax collector. I fast twice a week, I give tithes of all that I get." But the tax collector, standing far off, would not even lift up his eyes to heaven, but beat his breast, saying, "God, be merciful to me a sinner!" I tell you, this man went down to his house justified rather than the other; for every one who exalts himself will be humbled, but he who humbles himself will be exalted.'
>
> (Luke 18:9–14)

This is probably the parable in which most obviously nothing stands for something else. It needs little interpretation, provided we do not add notions which are foreign to it. We must therefore not look upon the Pharisee as insincere. The Pharisees were genuinely concerned about knowing God's will and carrying it out. They understood, quite rightly, that human righteousness consists in abiding by God's Covenant and therefore walking in his ways. God's ways are known. They were revealed in the Law, in the commandments. If sometimes the Pharisees' insistence on the importance of what seem to us minor details does not appeal to us, we should realize that this insistence was born from a very real desire to be obedient in all things—a very proper desire, for obedience up to a point is no obedience at all.

However, this Pharisee went a step further. There is no commandment about fasting twice a week, but fasting was regarded as a pious religious custom, and this man was obviously keen to please God in whatever way he could. His tithing too went beyond what the Law requires. Tithing as required by the Law was demanded of the producer, not the buyer of agricultural produce (Deuteronomy 14:22–9). But it was well known that not all farmers were as scrupulous about it as they should be. It was therefore always possible that some wheat or oil or whatever one bought had not been tithed at the source. That was really nobody's business but the offender's, but scrupulous people like this Pharisee religiously paid the tithes, one tenth of the value, of everything they bought, thus making up for the sins of others.

These people therefore had something to be proud of. They really did know the Law and carried it out, and even made up for the shortcomings of others. Yet this man was not really boasting. One might even call him humble. He regarded his outstanding religious achievements not as something that he had given to God, but as a privilege, something that God had given to him, and he thanked God for it. There are examples of similar prayers in the Talmud.

The tax collector (*publicanus*, a public servant, not a 'publican' as understood in common English usage) was not in a position to do the same. His job meant that he was in the service of the enemies of his people, clearly not the kind of thing that could be defined as 'walking within the Covenant'. Many tax collectors were also dishonest and extorted more money from people than was due, but that is not mentioned in this case. Also, being in Roman service meant regular contact with Gentiles, and therefore defilement according to the strictest interpretation of the Law. However, the important point is not which particular transgressions could be laid to his charge, but the simple fact that he was a sinner and knew it.

But what was the point of the story? Caird suggests that two men went up to the Temple to pray, but only one of them prayed. But the Lord does not, in fact, say that. Nor does he say that the Pharisee went home condemned. Even if we interpret the final sentence as meaning, 'This man went down to his house justified, and the other did not . . .', we must not put too much weight on the element of condemnation. What we can say is that the tax collector had received from his visit to the Temple something that the other had not received.

Yet there is a criticism of the Pharisee. It concerns the demarcation line that he had drawn between himself and the tax collector. God does not care for such demarcation lines. The tax collector is one of his own just as much as the other. He accepts him as he accepts the Pharisee. That is all the justification either of them needs.

Ultimately the Pharisee's attitude is dangerous because it creates a false security. He knows that he owes all that he has to God, and that even his piety is God's gift. But he is coming perilously near the stage where he will seek his security in those things which make him different from other people. His security does not in fact lie in his piety. His security, like the tax collector's, lies in God's mercy. The tax collector can never be sure of himself, but neither can he. But they can both be sure of God, who has accepted them for his own.

The two debtors

One of the Pharisees asked him to eat with him, and he went into the Pharisee's house, and sat at table. And behold, a woman of the city, who was a sinner, when she learned that he was sitting at table in the Pharisee's house, brought an alabaster flask of ointment, and standing behind him at his feet, weeping, she began to wet his feet with her tears, and wiped them with the hair of her head, and kissed his feet, and anointed them with the ointment. Now when the Pharisee who had invited him saw it, he said to himself, 'If this man were a prophet, he would have known who and what sort of woman this is who is touching him, for she is a sinner.'

And Jesus answering said to him,
'Simon, I have something to say to you.'
And he answered, 'What is it, Teacher?'

'A certain creditor had two debtors; one owed five hundred denarii, and the other fifty. When they could not pay, he forgave them both. Now which of them will love him more?'
Simon answered,
'The one, I suppose, to whom he forgave more.'
And he said to him,
'You have judged rightly.'
Then turning toward the woman he said to Simon,
'Do you see this woman? I entered your house, you gave me no water for my feet, but she has wet my feet with her tears and wiped them with her hair. You gave me no kiss, but from the time I came in she has not ceased to kiss my feet. You did not anoint my head with oil, but she has anointed my feet with ointment. Therefore I tell you, her sins, which are many, are forgiven, for she loved much; but he who is forgiven little, loves little.'
And he said to her,
'Your sins are forgiven.'
Then those who were at table with him began to say among themselves, *'Who is this, who even forgives sins?'*
And he said to the woman,
'Your faith has saved you; go in peace.'

(Luke 7:36–50)

This parable sits very tightly in its context, so much so that it seems almost indecent to ask if this is its original situation. True, the very similar situation of Mark 14:3–9 provoked a different reaction, but we must not overlook that in both cases the first reaction came from others, not from the Lord. In Mark 14 the extravagant act of the woman makes some people comment that the ointment could have been sold and the proceeds given to the poor; Jesus therefore has to defend the woman against those who measure everything in terms of money and cannot appreciate a spontaneous act of love. But here it is the woman's character that is at issue. We can no longer tell whether the two stories contain memories of different features of the same event. So much is certain that we must read each story as we find it.

If it is true that the Gospel is not something that can be abstracted from the stories, if, indeed, here as elsewhere in the Bible, the story is the message, it will be necessary to look at the story as a whole.

The first point to be noted is that Jesus is invited to have a meal at the house of a Pharisee. The Pharisees are still on speaking terms with him; they are inclined to regard him more or less as one of their own, and the Evangelist makes it clear that Jesus, for his part, looks upon Simon as a man who could be won over: he appeals to him—that is the point of the parable—and the issue is left open. We do not learn whether or not this Pharisee accepted the Gospel. That is none of our business. Our business is that the Lord offers the same challenge to us as to Simon.

The woman is simply referred to as 'a sinner'. We are not told what her sin was. The tradition has not been content with that and has asserted that she was a prostitute, but the fact is that we do not know. Forgiveness and repentance do not require that all sins are made public. Bonhoeffer once observed that some parsons tend to be like gutter press journalists: they want to see everyone naked, they want to ferret out all the hidden sins. There is nothing like that in the Lord's ministry. When the sins of the past are forgiven and swept away their memory is covered up. The Lord therefore just accepts the woman's rather extravagant and perhaps embarrassing act of gratitude and does not refer to her sins until Simon does.

Neither does the woman refer to them. She is more interested in her present joy than in her past sins. Actually that shows the genuineness of her repentance. Sometimes, when people keep going on and on about their past sins, one begins to wonder if perhaps they love them too much to give up their memory.

Thus neither the Lord nor the woman nor the Evangelist finds it necessary to give us the details. All that we need to know is that she knew her sins were forgiven—not even how she knew.

The parable itself is quite simple and its relevance to the situation quite obvious. Note that the two debtors are both in debt but not to the same amount. The point of the parable therefore is not that it makes no difference how we live. Jesus leaves no doubt that the Pharisees, in attempting to do God's will day by day and all day, are doing the right thing. Whatever differences there may have been between Jesus and the Pharisees, this is one thing on which they agreed: God's will is to be done. Their sincere attempts to understand God's will and to carry it out give the Pharisees a distinct advantage over those who make no such attempt. The Lord recognizes that there is a difference between the righteous and the open sinners, between the good and the wicked, between the pious and the ungodly.

But Simon's advantage can become a trap if he does not see that the difference is a relative difference. One debtor may owe more than the other but they are both in debt. Before God one person may have dirtier hands than another but they both need washing. One may be a greater sinner than another but they both need forgiveness. Simon is right to live his life by God's commandments but he still lives by God's grace and he is still dependent on God's goodness.

The contrast between Simon's cool reception of Jesus and the woman's exuberance shows her gratitude. There is a slight lack of clarity in verse 47: the grammar is rather loose, both in the Greek and in translation. The Lord obviously does not mean that her sins are forgiven because she loved much, but rather, that *one can see* that her sins are forgiven because she loves much; in other words, her love is evidence that she knows that she has been forgiven. The Lord then confirms what she already believed, already knew: 'Your sins are forgiven'.

As we observed before, the issue of the story is left open. Will Simon see that, no matter how different he and the woman are, no matter how much greater her sins may be, they have one thing in common? They are both in God's debt, they both live by God's grace.

7

The Joy of God

THE previous parable contained an important element additional to God's generosity. The woman whose action was the occasion of the parable had responded to God's grace with exuberant joy. A most natural reaction.

But we have now come to a number of parables with a much more incredible point: the joy of God. Who would believe it? God takes a delight in our salvation.

Is that speaking of God in terms too human? But then, we know God only as he has shown himself in Jesus Christ. Who would dare suggest that he is different from that which he has shown himself to be?

The lost sheep

'See that you do not despise one of these little ones; for I tell you that in heaven their angels always behold the face of my Father who is in heaven. What do you think? If a man has a hundred sheep, and one of them has gone astray, does he not leave the ninety-nine on the hills and go in search of the one that went astray? And if he finds it, truly, I say to you, he rejoices over it more than over the ninety-nine that never went astray. So it is not the will of my Father who is in heaven that one of these little ones should perish.'

(Matthew 18:10–14)

Now the tax collectors and sinners were all drawing near to hear him. And the Pharisees and the scribes murmured, saying, 'This man receives sinners and eats with them.'

So he told them this parable:

The Kingdom of God is Like This

'What man of you, having a hundred sheep, if he has lost one of them, does not leave the ninety-nine in the wilderness, and go after the one which is lost, until he finds it? And when he has found it, he lays it on his shoulders, rejoicing. And when he comes home, he calls together his friends and his neighbours, saying to them, "Rejoice with me, for I have found my sheep which was lost." Just so, I tell you, there will be more joy in heaven over one sinner who repents than over ninety-nine righteous persons who need no repentance.'

(Luke 15 : 1–7)

This well-known parable has come down to us in two versions put in entirely different contexts. Matthew 18 begins with the question, 'Who is the greatest in the kingdom of heaven?' to which the Lord replies, 'Truly, I say to you, unless you turn and become like children, you will never enter the kingdom of heaven. Whoever humbles himself like this child, he is the greatest in the kingdom of heaven.'

There follow some more sayings about children, ending with a warning not to put temptation in their way. The children in this passage could be meant in the literal sense, but Jesus could also be referring to believers who have become like children, or perhaps even to both.

The word temptation leads the Evangelist on to some other sayings about temptation (vv.7–9), but in verse 10 he returns to the children. No one should despise the little ones—which, again, could be meant either in the literal sense or as referring to the simple believers.

It is in this context that Matthew places the parable of the Lost Sheep. If a man has a hundred sheep, and one goes astray, what does he do? Of course, he goes and looks for it. Who would not? He forgets about the ninety-nine: he must have the one back! And when he finds it he rejoices over it more than over the ninety-nine that never went astray. Why? The parable does not say, but it is obvious: it is because he cares.

The point is equally obvious. If a mere human shepherd cares so much for what is, after all, only a sheep, will not God care much more for even the least of his children? Therefore, see to it that you do not despise one of these little ones.

Luke's context is different and seems more natural. Jesus is being criticized for the company he keeps. We have to understand the situation. The critics are the Pharisees and Scribes, and Luke seems to have been more aware than the other Evangelists that their attitude was not entirely hostile. They were opposed to him but at the same time they showed genuine concern. They were concerned mainly about two things. First of all, his friendship with tax collectors and other bad characters might get him a bad name and might also in the long run have a bad effect on his own conduct. You cannot work with muck without becoming dirty. He should choose his friends more carefully, for his own good.

But there was another point. The Pharisees knew perfectly well that God receives the repentant sinner and the sight of such a man sitting down in sackcloth and ashes would certainly have met with their approval. But Jesus received sinners and ate with them, as if repentance was a reason to throw a party!

So Jesus told them this parable.

Not only the context, the parable itself too is more natural in this Gospel. It evokes a complete picture and suggests even the details which it does not relate in so many words. We can see this shepherd as he counts his sheep and finds that there is one missing. We can see him setting out to find it, forgetting for the moment about the others; we can watch him searching and stopping short when he thinks he can hear it. Above all, we can see him coming home, his clothes torn and his feet bleeding, but he is whistling cheerfully, for he has his sheep on his shoulders; and when he meets a neighbour he shouts, 'I lost my sheep, but I have found it again! That calls for a celebration!'

What do you think? If a mere human shepherd wants to celebrate when he has found again what is, after all, only a sheep, how much greater must God's joy be over one sinner who repents.

It cannot be stressed too strongly that in both versions of the parable the shepherd is just a shepherd, and the sheep is just a sheep. Nothing stands for anything else. The point is precisely, and this gives the parable its proper weight and its compelling power of demonstration, that God is more than a human shepherd and that we are not sheep.

It is, of course, very tempting to overlook that. The shepherd is a very ancient figure of speech. Since days immemorial the Egyptian Pharaohs carried a shepherd's crook as a symbol of their office: they were the shepherds of their people. Similarly in Israel the leaders of the nation were sometimes referred to as shepherds. Above all, God is frequently regarded as the Shepherd of Israel (Psalms 23, 80 and elsewhere) and in John 10 Jesus refers to himself as the Good Shepherd.

But it is characteristic of this parable that no direct reference is made to such aspects. The picture of a shepherd taking good care of his animals would naturally remind the listeners of the Shepherd of Israel, but the story remains self-contained.

Allegorization of this parable can easily lead to rather odd interpretations. Thus, for instance, it has been argued that, as the parable mentions only the shepherd and the sheep, that is to say, God and the sinner, there is no need for a Mediator, and that this parable 'proves' by the Lord's own words, that the Christian teaching about the Cross is all wrong. Others have replied by saying that God is not mentioned in the parable: the shepherd stands for Jesus. But the whole controversy is pointless. The shepherd does not stand either for God or for Jesus, he is simply a shepherd.

Where the two versions differ is that Matthew has adapted this parable addressed to the Pharisees in such a manner that it could be used more readily as an appeal to Christians who were less than charitable to other Christians. Luke's version seems to be closer to the original. Jesus does not deny that the Pharisees are godly people. Indeed, they have much to commend them. But they must see that, just as it gives a shepherd joy when he finds a sheep which was lost, it gives God great joy —far greater joy—when one sinner repents.

No doubt Luke, in his own mind, expanded the scope of the parable. His thoughts would turn naturally to the admission of Gentiles to the people of God. That too is a cause of great joy to God. But in expanding the application he has retained the point of the story.

Matthew realized that the Pharisees are found not only in Israel but also in the Church. There are good Christians who do not want to make repentance too easy—perhaps also some godly people who are convinced that all people are sinners but somehow regard themselves as the exceptions that confirm the rule. This application of the parable is legitimate, indeed, it is inevitable. But somehow, in doing that, he has not focused sufficient attention on the joy of God. It is still mentioned but it does not receive the full light. Yet this is what the parable is really about: the joy of God. It is an invitation to share in that joy.

That is the great surprise of the Gospel. It is so easy to think of God as unconcerned. Even if we do speak of the love of God we tend to think of the Gospel in terms of a take-it-or-leave-it offer. Jesus wants us to see how deeply God has involved himself with us.

The end of the parable thus returns to the beginning, the comment that Jesus *eats* with publicans and sinners, with enemies of the nation and other bad characters. When the Lord finds a person, when he brings someone back to the family of God, that is a good reason to throw a party. What better reason could there be? What greater joy could there be for God than to receive one of his people back? What greater joy could there be for a sinner than to be accepted by God? God celebrates. The repentant sinner celebrates. We must all celebrate.

The invitation to celebrate is extended to all, but it is aimed specifically at the 'righteous persons who need no repentance'. It has been asked whether there are such persons and the obvious answer seems to be 'no'. It has therefore been suggested that the Lord meant the phrase ironically. There may, indeed, be an element of irony in it. Yet, though it may be true that all people have sinned, that does not mean that there are no distinctions. There is something absurd about the manner in which some people think it is godly to confess sins they have never committed—rather like the cranks who write a confession to Scotland Yard after every serious crime reported in the papers. When we are told—as is sometimes done in attempts at high-pressure evangelism—that 'we must all become murderers and thieves', the only healthy reaction is, to say, 'No, thank you!'

True, there is a sense, a very deep sense, in which we are all

91

sinners, in which we are all guilty before God. But we shall only realize that when we have encountered God's love in Christ, and it certainly does not mean that we must pretend that we have committed sins which, in fact, we have not committed.

Also, it is true that we are responsible for each other, responsible for each other's sins too. There is a solidarity of guilt from which no one escapes. But that is not what the Lord was thinking about at this particular moment.

He was speaking of the 'righteous persons who need no repentance'. Righteousness, in the Old Testament, does not mean moral perfection. A righteous person is someone who lives according to the Covenant. To be sure, that does imply that he tries to carry out God's commandments and to walk in his ways, but it does not mean that he is morally perfect.

It is therefore perfectly possible for people to be righteous in one sense. True, when they come to think of it and when they look at themselves critically, they will realize that their righteousness has its limits, that they too are guilty before God, that they too depend on God's generosity, on God's forgiving love. We saw that the Lord said as much in the parable of the Two Debtors. But that is not the issue of this parable.

This parable is an invitation, to all, but particularly to the righteous, to join in the joy of God. When a sinner repents, God celebrates. The repentant sinner celebrates. We must all celebrate.

The lost coin

> '*Or what woman, having ten silver coins, if she loses one coin, does not light a lamp and sweep the house and seek diligently until she finds it? And when she has found it, she calls together her friends and neighbours, saying, "Rejoice with me, for I have found the coin which I had lost." Just so, I tell you, there is joy before the angels of God over one sinner who repents.*'
>
> (Luke 15:8–10)

The first impression modern readers receive, when they read this parable after that of the Lost Sheep, is one of anticlimax. We cannot tell if Luke felt the same. A coin is of much less value than a sheep. Yet we all know the frantic search than can be made for even a small coin. If people make so much fuss about a coin, must not God be ready to take endless trouble over a human being? That is fine as far as it goes, but one would scarcely call in the neighbours to celebrate the finding of a 5p piece!

We shall probably therefore have to picture the silver coin as an heirloom, perhaps part of one of those chains of silver or gold coins oriental women still like to wear. Losing one of those coins is much more upsetting than the mere loss of the money. Try to picture the scene, perhaps a neighbour saying 'Look, your chain is broken!' The woman quickly picks up the coins —but there is one missing. So the house is turned upside down until the missing piece is found, and there she is, running next door with it in her hand, 'Look, I've found it!'

How natural that she is delighted. But, let us face it, a coin is only a coin, even if it is an heirloom and even if we value it beyond its face value. How much more delighted must God be over one sinner who repents!

The prodigal son

And he said,
'There was a man who had two sons; and the younger of them said to his father, "Father, give me the share of property that falls to me." And he divided his living between them. Not many days later, the younger son gathered all he had and took his journey into a far country, and there he squandered his property in loose living. And when he had spent everything a great famine arose in that country, and he began to be in want. So he went and joined himself to one of the citizens of that country, who sent him into his fields to feed swine. And he would gladly have fed on the pods that the swine ate; and no one gave him anything. But when he came to himself he said, "How many of my father's hired servants have bread enough and to spare, but I perish here with hunger! I will arise and go to my father, and I will say to him, Father, I have sinned against heaven and before you; I am no longer worthy to be called your son; treat me as one of your hired servants." And he arose and came to his father. But while he was yet at a distance, his father saw him and had compassion, and ran and embraced him and kissed him. And the son said to him, "Father, I have sinned against heaven and before you; I am no longer worthy to be called your son." But the father

*said to his servants, "Bring quickly the best robe, and put it on him;
and put a ring on his hand, and shoes on his feet; and bring the
fatted calf and kill it, and let us eat and make merry; for this my
son was dead, and is alive again; he was lost, and is found." And
they began to make merry.*

*'Now his elder son was in the field; and as he came and drew
near to the house, he heard music and dancing. And he called one
of the servants and asked what this meant. And he said to him,
"Your brother has come, and your father has killed the fatted calf,
because he has received him safe and sound." But he was angry and
refused to go in. His father came out and entreated him, but he
answered his father, "Lo, these many years I have served you, and
I never disobeyed your command; yet you never gave me a kid, that
I might make merry with my friends. But when this son of yours
came, who has devoured your living with harlots, you killed for him
the fatted calf!" And he said to him, "Son, you are always with me,
and all that is mine is yours. It was fitting to make merry and be
glad, for this your brother was dead, and is alive; he was lost, and is
found." '*

(Luke 15 : 11–32)

The Parable of the Prodigal Son has been attached by Luke to
those of the Lost Sheep and the Lost Coin, and rightly so,
because its main purpose is very similar.

However, there are some significant differences between this
parable and the two others. For one thing, whereas the sheep
was merely foolish (but then, it was only a sheep!), and the
coin was just lost, the younger son in this parable is guilty. Of
course, that is simply the outcome of the fact that this parable
speaks of a human being. Coins and sheep cannot be guilty;
sons can. But this does bring the son in much closer proximity
to the sinners found in the Lord's company.

Also, the second part of the parable pays much more attention to the elder son than the other parables did to the ninety-
nine sheep and the nine coins that were not lost. But again,
that is simply because the Lord is here speaking of human
beings. Sheep and coins cannot protest, sons can. However, it
does bring the elder son very close to the pious Israelites who
protested against our Lord's fellowship with sinners.

It is therefore extremely tempting to treat this parable as an
allegory. That temptation is encouraged by certain minor
features of the story. Thus, for instance, the way in which the

father gives in to the younger son's request and sets him at liberty to do as he pleases reminds us of the way in which God lets men out on a very long and very thin leash, so long and so thin that it might seem that we can move away entirely beyond his reach. It does seem at times that God is very remote, so remote that those who want to find him have a long way to go; so remote that many people believe there is no God.

But the father sees him while he was yet at a distance: God sees us when we think he is far away, and he is ready to meet us.

Also, the son never has the opportunity to say all that he had to say. The father does not want him back as a hired servant, he wants him for a son, and the boy is not given the chance to become otherwise. He is spared the final humiliation of being a servant in his own home. Similarly, it is natural for the sinner to humble himself before God, but God does not desire his final humiliation. Perhaps man expects the worst when he comes before God, for he does not yet know God's generosity, but God wants the sinner as his own child, not as a mere servant.

Finally, the elder brother is very reminiscent of those good and religious people who try to do God's will but always seem to have a grudge: 'Lo, these many years I have served you, and I never disobeyed your command. . . .' They do not know that the service of God is perfect freedom. They carry out religiously all that God requires, but they do not enjoy it. They try to avoid sin but secretly think, 'What a pity this or that is a sin!'

All these observations are true enough. And yet it would be a mistake to treat this parable as an allegory. The story is a straightforward yarn, and nothing 'stands for something else'. The most that one can say is that several features remind us of something else, or, more precisely, of the relationship between God and us. But the father in the parable is very definitely not God. God too may seem to give us more freedom than we know how to cope with, but he is not as foolish as the father in the parable. Also, we feel that the father, much though we admire his treatment of the younger son at his return, had been less than generous to the elder, to whom he never even gave a kid to make merry with his friends. Like all men this father had his faults—he was bound to, for, after all, he was just an ordinary father. In fact, it is quite possible that Jesus did not invent the story but that something like that had actually happened in the town where he told the parable.

The story then is quite straightforward. A man of some wealth has two sons, and the younger asks him if he can have his share of the inheritance now, rather than after the father's death. The request is granted, and the son leaves home to enjoy the lights of the city. We need not take it for granted that he spent his money on slow horses and fast women—his brother was later to assume the worst, but, of course, he did not actually know—but he did manage to work through his money pretty quickly: it is amazing how much money you can spend in how little time if you really try!

He would have had plenty of 'friends' while he was still busy spending but they disappeared rapidly as soon as his funds ran out, and in the end he was reduced to accepting any job that was going. Imagine what a Jew must have felt at having to feed pigs!

Hunger in the end brought him to his senses. He knew that he had no longer any rights at home: the entire estate would pass in due time to his brother. But he might at least be able to find a job there and enough to eat. So he went home.

But his father would not have him as a mere servant. He was glad to have his son back. A great surprise for the boy, though not for the listeners. They would have been deeply shocked if the father had reacted in any other way. The family means a great deal in Jewish life, and the people who heard Jesus must have expected that the father would act in the way he did. It is important that we realize that, for only then will we grasp the point. If a mere human father, any human father, will gladly have his prodigal son back, will God not be equally glad, if not more so?

On the other hand, the behaviour of the other son would have been felt to be unnatural. He may perhaps have had some genuine reason to grouse, but this was not the time. His brother had come back, and that was a cause for celebration. Why, even the ungodly Esau, whose brother Jacob had treated him so shabbily and deceived him so treacherously, was genuinely pleased to see his brother again (Genesis chapters 27 and 33)!

Well now, if it is unnatural for a brother to resent the celebrations at the return of the prodigal, is it not much more unnatural for a faithful child of God not to be genuinely glad when a sinner repents?

Note that the end of the parable is left open, like one of those modern plays of which people complain that they have no proper ending. We are not told whether the elder brother listened to his father and joined the party in the end. No doubt that was deliberate. The story was just a story, but ultimately the Lord wanted to appeal to his listeners. They were invited to join God's party. They had to give an answer.

When we speak of 'God's party' we are, of course, referring specifically to such occasions as the party given by Levi to celebrate his new friendship with Jesus (Luke 5:29). That, after all, was the kind of thing the Lord's critics had in mind (Luke 5:30; 15:2); it was also the kind of celebration the Lord wanted them to join. But the application is much wider. When a man finds out about God's generous love, that is a cause of great joy. It calls for a celebration. God celebrates. The repentant sinners celebrate. We must all celebrate.

The man without festive clothes

'... But when the king came in to look at the guests, he saw there a man who had no wedding garment; and he said to him, "Friend, how did you get in here without a wedding garment?" And he was speechless. Then the king said to the attendants, "Bind him hand and foot, and cast him into the outer darkness; there men will weep and gnash their teeth." For many are called, but few are chosen.'

(Matthew 22:11-14)

Matthew has attached this short parable to that of the Excuses (Matthew 22:1-10; see p. 43). In this context it is simply a continuation of the other, and, of course, we cannot dismiss altogether the possibility that the Lord may at times have told parables in this way, one following from the other. However, it is obvious that Matthew has to some extent allegorized the story: when people are thrown out of a house they do not normally arrive at the place where men weep and gnash their teeth.

It is usually assumed that Matthew, in these verses, wanted to correct to some extent a misunderstanding that might arise from the preceding parable and from the Lord's attitude to sinners. It is not enough to hear the invitation and accept it. There must be a further response consisting of right conduct. Conversion must lead to good works. Many are called, but few are chosen, that is to say, few will be found worthy. The Lord will examine his people at the Last Judgment, and only then shall we know who are worthy.

Another interpretation is suggested by a similar parable attributed to a first century rabbi. This describes a king who had sent invitations for a feast but had given no time. The wise dressed themselves for the occasion, the foolish went on with their work. Suddenly the final invitation came, and those who were not dressed properly were not allowed in. In this case the interpretation is given too. The festive clothes point to repentance, and repentance is demanded now, for no one knows the hour of his death, and then it will be too late. It has been suggested that Jesus may have told his parable with the same intention.

However, we must ask, are these really natural interpretations of the parable? When people first heard it, whether by itself or as a sequel to the parable of the Excuses, what would a wedding garment, what would festive clothes have suggested? Good works? Repentance? Surely the most natural, the only natural thing suggested by festive clothes is festivity, celebration, joy, fun. The criticism levelled regularly at our Lord was that sinners enjoyed his company and he seemed to enjoy theirs; 'This man receives sinners and eats with them.'

Christ brings the joy of God. True, following Christ also leads to hardship, sometimes to persecution, and it certainly entails making sacrifices. It could not be otherwise, as we are following a crucified Lord. Yet, the first thing he offers is the joy that comes from being accepted by God, from being at peace with God.

The Gospel according to John emphasizes this by attaching

so much importance to the wine miracle of Cana, which he calls the first sign that Jesus did (John 2 : 11)—and he does not just mean that it was the first in order of time or the first in his narrative. This was the principal of his signs, and also the principle underlying all his work: he turns the tasteless water of drab everyday life into the wine of glorious living with God. It is significant that this is the sign, that Jesus made sure at a country wedding that the fun of the party was not spoiled.

If that is what the Lord had in mind—and, honestly, is that not what the festive clothes suggest?—then this parable is aimed at those who want to make the service of God into hard servitude, those who spoil the joy of God both for themselves and for others. They speak of salvation and great joy but look as miserable as sin.

The parable was then, at the time, spoken with specific reference to the religious leaders of Israel. Their trouble was not that they were not serious about the service of God. On the contrary, they were too serious. They took themselves too seriously because they did not know the joy of God.

But if we think that this is merely an interesting bit of information we must remind ourselves that the parable is aimed also at those who hear it now. Nietzsche once observed, 'They must sing better songs before I can learn to believe in their Saviour; his disciples must look like people who were saved.' There is often so little joy in religion. Meeting Christ is the opportunity to be saved from such religion, to be saved from our solemnity and to learn the joy of God.

8

The Way of Life

TAKING the great chance offered in Jesus Christ, receiving God's infinite generosity, means salvation. But what does Christ do with those whom he has saved? We have already seen part of the answer: he celebrates. He celebrates with us, we celebrate with him, we are made to share in God's joy.

But there is another side. The Christian life is lived in the joy of God, but it is also lived in a world with many problems and conflicts. There are not many parables dealing with that side of the Christian life, at least, not many have come down to us. That may seem surprising, but actually it should not surprise us. The parables, as we have seen, are usually not general but specific. They refer to specific situations in which Christ met people—and meets people. That means that, if our Lord did tell parables concerned with moral questions, they would refer to specific situations, and therefore be highly relevant at the time when they were told, but less so in other situations. They would therefore be less likely to be remembered. Life is infinitely varied, well, almost infinitely. Every situation is different, and every situation demands new and original decisions. Obedience to a living Master, a risen Lord, means precisely not to abide by unchangeable rules and to follow eternally valid examples but to find out what he requires in the new situations in which we find ourselves.

However, a number of sayings of Jesus on everyday conduct were remembered and have survived; also some parables. Even if every situation is new, there are at times obvious parallels.

The Kingdom of God is Like This

Sometimes we can recognize ourselves in situations of the past; we can also recognize ourselves in the people whom Jesus met when he was in the flesh. Such cases can help us very much indeed to come to know what he wants us to do. The early Church has had a keen eye for that and has preserved what seemed relevant.

The two houses

'Every one then who hears these words of mine and does them will be like a wise man who built his house upon the rock; and the rain fell, and the floods came, and the winds blew and beat upon that house, but it did not fall, because it had been founded on the rock. And every one who hears these words of mine and does not do them will be like a foolish man who built his house upon the sand; and the rain fell, and the floods came, and the winds blew and beat against that house, and it fell; and great was the fall of it.'

(Matthew 7: 24–7)

'Why do you call me "Lord, Lord," and not do what I tell you? Every one who comes to me and hears my words and does them, I will show you what he is like: he is like a man building a house, who dug deep, and laid the foundation upon rock; and when a flood arose, the stream broke against that house, and could not shake it, because it had been well built. But he who hears and does not do them is like a man who built a house on the ground without a foundation; against which the stream broke, and immediately it fell, and the ruin of that house was great.'

(Luke 6: 46–9)

This parable has been handed down by both Matthew and Luke in very much the same context. They both place it at the end of a long sermon; Matthew at the end of the Sermon on the Mount (Matthew 5–7) and Luke at the end of the Sermon on the Plain (Luke 6: 17–49), which is in many ways the Lucan equivalent; and both connect it with a saying about those who address the Lord in the most reverent terms but do not do as he tells them (Matthew 7: 21–3; Luke 6: 46). It seems therefore likely that they found the parable in the source known as 'Q' in very much the same context.

That makes it all the more remarkable that the parable itself varies so much in detail in the two Gospels. The Evangelists were apparently more concerned to repeat it in a form which the readers would be able to understand than to retain the precise wording. The variations must be attributed to conditions in the countries where the two Gospels were written. They do not affect the point that the parable wants to make.

But what about the context? Is it likely to be original? The two sermons are compositions by the Evangelists, obviously dependent on a sermon in the source 'Q' that was itself composite and made up of originally unconnected sayings and stories. There is therefore no guarantee that the Lord had told the story in view of those who called him, 'Lord, Lord,' but did not do as he told them. But it is difficult to see in what other context he could have told it. Moreover, the connexion is quite specific, and, as we saw, it is characteristic of the Lord's parables that they do not illustrate a general truth but refer to a specific situation.

That situation here is the encounter with himself. The parable does not speak of a contrast between those who only listen and those who act on what they have heard. It contrasts those who listen to Jesus, perhaps with great respect, perhaps even with approval, but do not actually follow him, with those who not only listen but draw the consequences, follow him, and do as he tells them.

This is therefore one of those parables in which Jesus makes it clear that the encounter with him is the critical moment. Not to recognize that is foolish, as foolish as building a house on drifting sands or marshy grounds without proper foundation.

But there is an added point. The decision for Christ is a matter not of words only but of obedience. It is not enough to give him the most exalted names and to approve of what he says. It is not even enough to have the most sincere and heartfelt reverence for him. Faith is a matter of obedience.

The Evangelists no doubt connected that obedience with the sermons of which the parable is the conclusion. However, that connexion was not there when the parable was first told, or even when it was handed down in the tradition. Jesus himself was referring to the guidance he was giving those who followed him; and the early Church was thinking not only in terms of the various sayings of Jesus but also of the guidance which the risen and living Lord was still giving day by day throughout the Spirit. Listening to what Jesus said while he was in the flesh, and hearing what he has to say now through the Spirit are both valid ways of learning to know the mind of Christ. But the Christian life is not only a matter of hearing and knowing his will. It is a matter of doing as he tells us, a matter of obdience.

However, it is obedience not just to anyone but to someone who is reliable, the One who can be trusted absolutely, Jesus Christ.

The two sons

'What do you think? A man had two sons; and he went to the first and said, "Son, go and work in the vineyard today." And he answered, "I will not", but afterward he repented and went. And he went to the second and said the same; and he answered, "I go, sir," but did not go. "Which of the two did the will of his father?" They said, 'The first.'

Jesus said to them,

'Truly, I say to you, the tax collectors and the harlots go into the kingdom of God before you. For John came to you in the way of righteousness, and you did not believe him, but the tax collectors and the harlots believed him; and even when you saw it, you did not afterward repent and believe him.' (Matthew 21 : 28–32)

It is very tempting to interpret this parable in a general sense. The story depicts a familiar scene. One often sees in a family that some of the children, whenever they are asked to do something say, 'no' but then do as they were asked, whilst others will always say, 'yes' but never do anything. The same is true of people in general. We are all familiar with the people who will do anything, everything, for us, but never actually do it, whilst others, though they may seem very unwilling, always end up by lending a hand when needed.

As we shall see, that interpretation, with its emphasis on the contrast between saying and doing, has a point. But it tempts us to overlook the more precise and specific side of the parable.

The Evangelist has not fallen for that temptation. He has realised that the application is not general but specific. It refers to the concrete encounter with God's will in a specific situation.

In the context in which it is here presented that specific situation is the ministry of John the Baptist. It was so easy for the pious in Israel to say that they were prepared to do God's will. But what did they do when they were confronted with the last of the prophets, John the Baptist? Did they repent? Were they not, in fact, far less obedient than many disreputable characters who made no pretence at godliness but repented when John put God's claim before them?

The connexion with John the Baptist seems a bit odd, and it seems fair to ask if Matthew has placed the parable in the right context. Was the Lord really referring to people's reaction to John, when he first told this parable, or was he referring to the decision they had to make when confronted with himself? We cannot be certain. The important decision, the decision that really matters is the one people make when they are confronted with Jesus Christ. But the context in which Matthew has presented this parable is a reminder that the encounter with Christ is sometimes mediated through his messenger.

However, it has been suggested that the original intention of the parable had nothing to do with any decision for either John or Jesus, but only with the contrast between saying and doing. If that is meant in a general sense, the suggestion must be refuted. But, of course, the parable does imply that the proper response to the will of God is not merely listening, or even saying 'yes', but obedience. The will of God is to be put into action.

Therefore, without emphasizing unduly the connexion with John, which may not be original, the parable speaks of the proper response to God's claim on us as and when it is made. The encounter with God's will demands a decision, and that means, action. Words alone are not enough. Faith implies obedience.

The unforgiving servant

> *Then Peter came up and said to him, 'Lord, how often shall my brother sin against me, and I forgive him? As many as seven times?'*
> *Jesus said to him,*
> *'I do not say to you seven times, but seventy times seven.*
> *'Therefore the kingdom of heaven may be compared to a king who wished to settle accounts with his servants. When he began the reckoning, one was brought to him who owed him ten thousand talents; and as he could not pay, his lord ordered him to be sold, with*

his wife and children and all that he had, and payment to be made. So the servant fell on his knees, imploring him, "Lord, have patience with me, and I will pay you everything." And out of pity for him the lord of that servant released him and forgave him the debt. But that same servant, as he went out, came upon one of his fellow servants who owed him a hundred denarii; and seizing him by the throat he said, "Pay what you owe." So his fellow servant fell down and besought him. "Have patience with me, and I will pay you." He refused and went and put him in prison till he should pay the debt. When his fellow servants saw what had taken place, they were greatly distressed, and they went and reported to their lord all that had taken place. Then his lord summoned him and said to him, "You wicked servant I forgave you all that debt because you besought me; and should not you have had mercy on your fellow servant, as I had mercy on you?" And in anger his lord delivered him to the jailers, till he should pay all his debt. So also my heavenly Father will do to every one of you, if you do not forgive your brother from your heart.' (Matthew 18:21–35)

This parable has certain similarities with that of the Two Debtors in Luke 7:36–50, but the differences are too great to regard them as different forms of the same parable. As in most cases, we cannot be certain that the context in which the Evangelist has placed this parable is the one in which it was first spoken, but it is a suitable context, which helps to bring out the point of the parable. Of course, it does not really answer Peter's question, 'How often shall my brother sin against me, and I forgive him?'; but then, a person who is genuinely willing to forgive does not count.

The story itself is quite straightforward, though it moves outside the normal range of the Lord's parables. The king is pictured as a very grand monarch indeed, not like one of the petty kings of the Herodian family but more like the Persian Great Kings of old, or perhaps the Caesar in Rome, and the 'servant' who owes him something like £5 000 000 must be pictured as the governor of a large and prosperous territory. While in office he has managed to squander a considerable part of the province's revenue, probably for his own pleasure, though evidently not for his own benefit; at any rate, he has 'borrowed' from the treasury, and he has no money to pay back.

The penalty is severe, but when he appeals to the king's mercy he is pardoned. Of course, his promise to pay everything back is ludicrous: where is a destitute man to find all that money? However, the king allows mercy to prevail.

Imagine his anger when he discovers that the same man with whom he has been so generous has a fellow servant, a minor government official, jailed for a paltry debt of about five pounds!

The point of the story is obvious. Those who owe so much to God's generosity and forgiveness ought to show the same generosity, ought to extend the same forgiveness, to others.

As in all the parables we must be careful not to decode the features of the story. The king is not God: he is just a king, a pagan at that who does not know God's law (the sale of a debtor's wife was prohibited in Israel), but people can sometimes be unexpectedly generous. Such generosity can be expected to lead to a response: it should make the recipient equally, or, at least, similarly generous. How much more must the generosity of almighty God evoke the response of our generosity!

The only secondary feature that can be used in the interpretation of the parable is the enormous difference between the two debts. Not seeing that difference betrays an extraordinary lack of a sense of proportion. We have everything out of proportion if we do not realize how little the hurt is which other people may have done us compared to the weight of our guilt before God. Nothing that people may have done to us, nothing for which they may need our forgiveness, can count for anything when we compare it with what God has forgiven us.

That is a fair inference from the parable, and, of course, it is directly related to Peter's question. However, the intention of the parable goes further and deeper than that, beyond counting and measuring. The Lord speaks of forgiving from the heart, of that genuine generosity that is born from God's own generosity and cannot do other than multiply and be fruitful.

The good Samaritan

And behold, a lawyer stood up to put him to the test, saying, 'Teacher, what shall I do to inherit eternal life?'
He said to him, 'What is written in the law? How do you read?'

And he answered, 'You shall love the Lord your God with all your heart, and with all your soul, and with all your strength, and with all your mind; and your neighbour as yourself.'

And he said to him, 'You have answered right; do this, and you will live.'

But he, desiring to justify himself, said to Jesus, 'And who is my neighbour?'

Jesus replied,

'A man was going down from Jerusalem to Jericho, and he fell among robbers, who stripped him and beat him, and departed, leaving him half-dead. Now by chance a priest was going down that road; and when he saw him he passed by on the other side. So likewise a Levite, when he came to the place and saw him, passed by on the other side. But a Samaritan, as he journeyed, came to where he was; and when he saw him, he had compassion, and went to him and bound up his wounds, pouring on oil and wine; then he set him on his own beast and brought him to an inn, and took care of him. And the next day he took out two denarii and gave them to the innkeeper, saying, "Take care of him; and whatever more you spend, I will repay you when I come back." Which of these three, do you think, proved neighbour to the man who fell among the robbers?'

He said, 'The one who showed mercy on him.'

And Jesus said to him, 'Go and do likewise.' (Luke 10:25–37)

As so often Luke provides a specific context for this parable. Two objections have been raised against this particular context. In the first place that the teacher of the law ('lawyer') gives the summary of the Law that Mark and Matthew attribute to Jesus himself (Mark 12:28–31; Matthew 22:34–9). However, there is some evidence that the rabbis had already reached the conclusion that the whole of the Law could be summed up in the commandment of love. It is not unlikely that the question came up more than once, and on one occasion the Lord supplied the answer and on another he left it to someone else to give it.

The other objection is that the parable does not really answer the question, 'Who is my neighbour?' If we want to be very precise, verse 37a seems to suggest that the Samaritan is the neighbour who should be loved; but in the second part of that verse, this same Samaritan is rather an example of a man who loved his neighbour.

However, the whole point of the parable is that the Lord does not want to answer the question, at least not as required by the teacher of the Law. The question implies that the term 'neighbour' limits the scope of love; the Law says that we must love our neighbour: now it is necessary to find out exactly who that neighbour is. The neighbour is surely not everybody, for we cannot be required to love everybody!? God's Law is specific!

To some extent the teacher of the Law had a point. God's Law is specific. It is so easy to love mankind and to hate people. Love of mankind is an abstraction that can easily blind us to the significance of people as people. But our neighbour is concrete and specific: it is that man with his record player making a row when we want some quiet, with that cat that keeps us awake at night or with that dog that fouls our front lawn. Even though the original Hebrew and Greek do not refer specifically to the man next door, it is still true to say that God's Law is deliberately concrete and specific.

Therefore the legalistic mind wants a definition: it wants to be absolutely certain who does and who does not come within the category of 'neighbour'. After all, we would not like to offend God by not extending our love to someone who is our neighbour and whom he wants us to love; on the other hand we do not want to waste our love on someone who is not our neighbour and whom we do not have to love!

The parable refuses to give such a definition. Instead it shows love in action, the kind of love that asks no questions.

The road from Jerusalem to Jericho was infested with marauding bands of partisans, usually referred to in the New Testament as 'robbers'. Their aim was to do as much harm to the Romans as possible, but wealthy Jewish travellers were not always safe from their predatory attentions. Thus, this traveller, a Jew, of course, was set upon by one of those bands, robbed, beaten up, and left half-dead. But help was close at hand—or was it? A priest was travelling down the road. He was by any definition a 'neighbour', and the victim was his 'neighbour'. But he passed by. So did a Levite who came down the road a little later. We are not given any reasons: the listeners are left to guess. Was it because they thought the man was dead and they did not want to defile themselves (after all they would have to do duty at the Temple again)? Or were they afraid that the robbers might still be lurking in the vicinity and they wanted to save their own skin? Or did they simply not care? Whatever their reason, the plain fact was that they did nothing.

Another man arrives at the spot. He is a Samaritan; not only an alien, but worse, an enemy of the Jewish nation. He does not think, he just sees. He sees a man who needs him, and acts spontaneously, giving first aid, taking the man to the nearest inn and paying his expenses. He does not fuss but just attends to what is needed.

And now the point of the story. Who is the neighbour? The victim of the assault, when he realized who had saved him, would have some thinking to do. Would he have accepted help from one of those cursed Samaritans if he had had a choice? Probably not. But at a time of real need he had found a neighbour where he least expected one.

And what about the teacher of the Law? He had not received an answer to his question. But he had been shown the example of a man who had not asked who his neighbour was; he had simply loved him.

The parable does not really go any further. But it was perhaps natural that sooner or later it should occur to some Christian preacher that Jesus Christ himself became our neighbour, that he set aside all other thoughts and did all that was necessary to save us. The story thus became a parable of the love of Christ. That is legitimate up to a point—but only up to a point. The love of the neighbour was not only preached by Christ: it was lived by him. He lived that perfect life of love that made him the man for others. The love that matters most in the Christian fellowship is the love of Christ for us. We love because he loved us first.

But it becomes a misinterpretation if it makes us forget that the Lord told this parable to show what our love should be like. It shows us a life in which people act without asking unprofitable questions, in which they give gladly what is needed, and receive gladly what is gladly given.

This love is quite unsentimental. It is not a matter of feeling deeply about someone else's distress or feeling grateful for somebody else's kindness. It is not even a matter of acting from the right motives. It is a matter of seeing people as we meet them, dealing with situations as they arise, giving the neighbour what he needs, whether it be first aid or money or just our attention or whatever it may be, and accepting what others are pleased to give.

All this comment may perhaps seem superfluous, as this parable is as plain today as it was when Jesus first told it. However, in all honesty we must point out that our comments are already application rather than interpretation. The story is simply a story. It serves as an illustration, but it neither explains nor defines anything, nor does it give an answer to any questions. But then the Christian life is not a matter of asking the right questions, nor even of finding the right answers. Life is to be lived, and the love of neighbour becomes real only in action.